Contents

Welcome to the Business, Administration and Finance Diploma!

The Business, Administration and Finance Diploma is a ground-breaking qualification created by employers, the Government and the leading education bodies. The Diploma will give you skills and experience that employers value and will provide you with opportunities to progress on to further studies.

The Diploma will introduce you to a broad range of topics relevant to the real world of business including marketing and sales, customer service, communication, personal finance and financial services, business administration and accounting.

You will learn how to develop new business ideas, and will be given the opportunity to develop and run your own business. You will learn about the issues affecting businesses today such as new technologies and environmental issues, and what businesses should do to remain competitive. This Diploma will equip you with knowledge on how businesses work and the skills you need to work in the business sector.

You will cover three main themes:

- **Business enterprise:** How to develop ideas, how to carry out research and promote products or services.
- **Business administration:** Introduces business administration and its importance to organisations.
- **Finance:** Looks at the knowledge and skills needed to manage personal and business finances.

Get stuck in!

The Foundation Diploma is equivalent to 5 GCSEs at level 1 (e.g. 5 GCSEs at grades D-G) and includes the following elements:

Principal learning The knowledge, understanding and skills essential to working in the Business sector, covered by this book.

Generic learning Functional skills in IT, English and mathematics, and personal learning and thinking skills (PLTS) have been embedded in this book to give you opportunities to develop and practise your skills.

The Project You will complete a business-related Project to demonstrate the skills and knowledge that you have learnt.

Additional/specialist learning You can choose from more than 800 different qualifications to support your Business principal learning. You might choose something that will further support you in a career in business, or something that relates to your other interests in order to broaden your skills.

Work experience Your Diploma will give you the opportunity to do at least 10 days' work experience. You should consider which local companies may be willing to offer you work experience as early as possible.

Going further

This Diploma is available at Foundation (Level 1, equivalent to 5 GCSEs at grades D–G), Higher (Level 2, equivalent to 7 GCSEs at grades A*–C) and Advanced (Level 3, equivalent to 3.5 A Levels at grades A*–E). The Advanced Diploma is recognised by universities and you could achieve up to 420 UCAS points.

From the Foundation Diploma, you can progress to:

- Higher Diploma
- BTEC First or other Level 2 vocational courses
- Apprenticeship
- GCSEs
- Work

We hope you enjoy your studies on this cutting-edge course and that you feel inspired by the real-life scenarios in this book. Good luck!

About this book

This book has been divided into five units to match the structure of the Principal Learning for the Foundation Diploma in Business, Administration and Finance.

Features of the book

There is a chapter devoted to every unit, and each chapter opens with the following:

- Overview – a description of what is covered in the unit
- Learning Outcomes and Topics list – a checklist of the Learning Outcomes covered in the unit, and how these relate to the topics covered
- Assessment – a short description of how the unit will be assessed

Each unit follows the Edexcel learning outcomes and each topic covers an individual theme.

Let's Get Going

A discussion point or short activity that will introduce the key concepts of the topic.

@work

These activities help you to think about how your learning could be applied during your work placement.

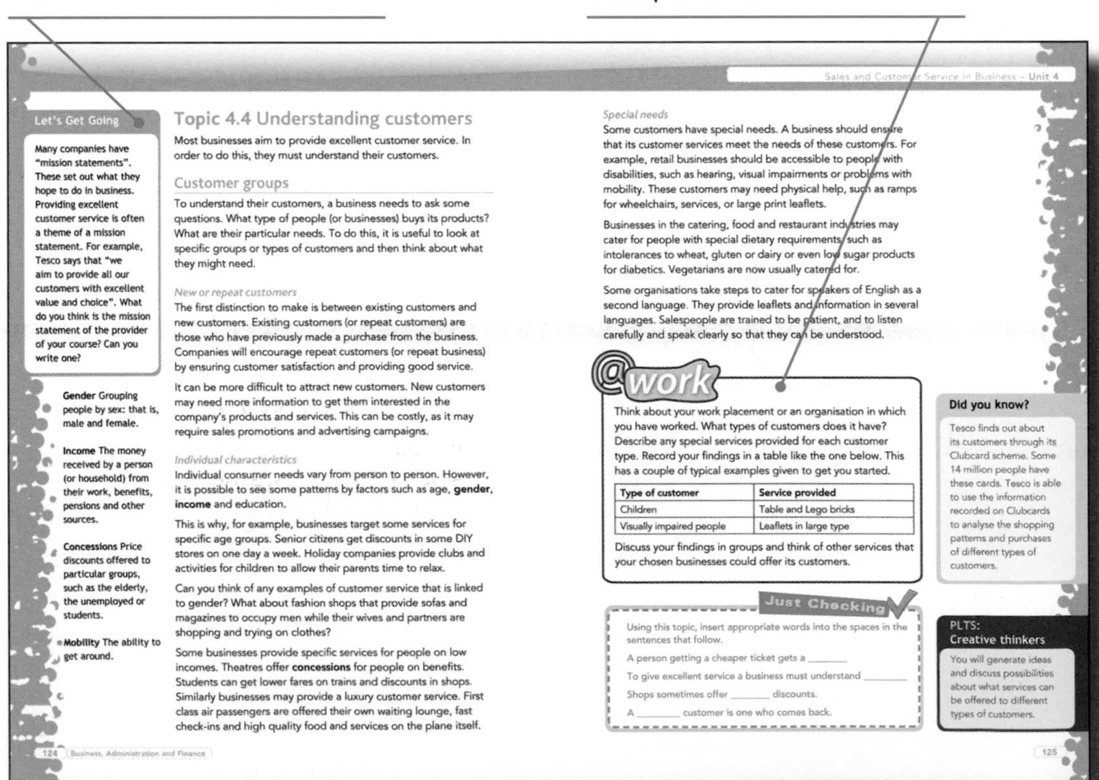

Let's Get Going

Many companies have "mission statements". These set out what they hope to do in business. Providing excellent customer service is often a theme of a mission statement. For example, Tesco says that "we aim to provide all our customers with excellent value and choice". What do you think is the mission statement of the provider of your course? Can you write one?

Gender Grouping people by sex: that is, male and female.

Income The money received by a person (or household) from their work, benefits, pensions and other sources.

Concessions Price discounts offered to particular groups, such as the elderly, the unemployed or students.

Mobility The ability to get around.

Topic 4.4 Understanding customers

Most businesses aim to provide excellent customer service. In order to do this, they must understand their customers.

Customer groups

To understand their customers, a business needs to ask some questions. What type of people (or businesses) buys its products? What are their particular needs. To do this, it is useful to look at specific groups or types of customers and then think about what they might need.

New or repeat customers

The first distinction to make is between existing customers and new customers. Existing customers (or repeat customers) are those who have previously made a purchase from the business. Companies will encourage repeat customers (or repeat business) by ensuring customer satisfaction and providing good service.

It can be more difficult to attract new customers. New customers may need more information to get them interested in the company's products and services. This can be costly, as it may require sales promotions and advertising campaigns.

Individual characteristics

Individual consumer needs vary from person to person. However, it is possible to see some patterns by factors such as age, **gender**, **income** and education.

This is why, for example, businesses target some services for specific age groups. Senior citizens get discounts in some DIY stores on one day a week. Holiday companies provide clubs and activities for children to allow their parents time to relax.

Can you think of any examples of customer service that is linked to gender? What about fashion shops that provide sofas and magazines to occupy men while their wives and partners are shopping and trying on clothes?

Some businesses provide specific services for people on low incomes. Theatres offer **concessions** for people on benefits. Students can get lower fares on trains and discounts in shops. Similarly businesses may provide a luxury customer service. First class air passengers are offered their own waiting lounge, fast check-ins and high quality food and services on the plane itself.

Special needs

Some customers have special needs. A business should ensure that its customer services meet the needs of these customers. For example, retail businesses should be accessible to people with disabilities, such as hearing, visual impairments or problems with mobility. These customers may need physical help, such as ramps for wheelchairs, services, or large print leaflets.

Businesses in the catering, food and restaurant industries may cater for people with special dietary requirements, such as intolerances to wheat, gluten or dairy or even low sugar products for diabetics. Vegetarians are now usually catered for.

Some organisations take steps to cater for speakers of English as a second language. They provide leaflets and information in several languages. Salespeople are trained to be patient, and to listen carefully and speak clearly so that they can be understood.

@work

Think about your work placement or an organisation in which you have worked. What types of customers does it have? Describe any special services provided for each customer type. Record your findings in a table like the one below. This has a couple of typical examples given to get you started.

Type of customer	Service provided
Children	Table and Lego bricks
Visually impaired people	Leaflets in large type

Discuss your findings in groups and think of other services that your chosen businesses could offer its customers.

Did you know?

Tesco finds out about its customers through its Clubcard scheme. Some 14 million people have these cards. Tesco is able to use the information recorded on Clubcards to analyse the shopping patterns and purchases of different types of customers.

Just Checking

Using this topic, insert appropriate words into the spaces in the sentences that follow.

A person getting a cheaper ticket gets a _______

To give excellent service a business must understand _______

Shops sometimes offer _______ discounts.

A _______ customer is one who comes back.

PLTS: Creative thinkers

You will generate ideas and discuss possibilities about what services can be offered to different types of customers.

Activity

These features contain an activity or a short sequence of questions to test your understanding and give you the opportunity to apply your knowledge and skills.

Personal learning and thinking skills (PLTS)

These features highlight opportunities to develop and demonstrate your personal learning and thinking skills.

Functional skills

These features highlight opportunities to develop and practise your functional skills in English, IT or mathematics. Remember, you will need a Pass in all three functional skills to achieve the full Diploma.

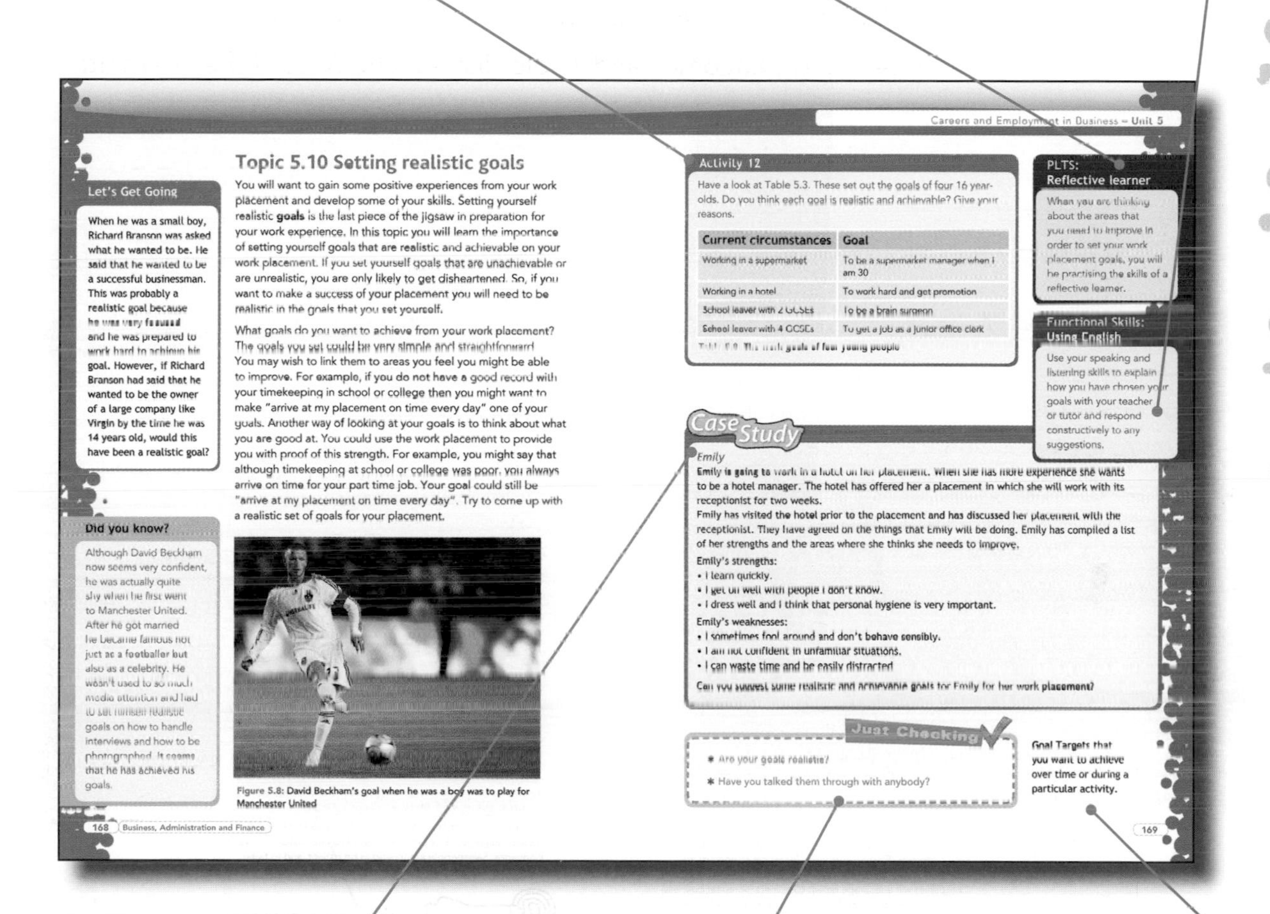

Careers and Employment in Business – Unit 5

Topic 5.10 Setting realistic goals

You will want to gain some positive experiences from your work placement and develop some of your skills. Setting yourself realistic **goals** is the last piece of the jigsaw in preparation for your work experience. In this topic you will learn the importance of setting yourself goals that are realistic and achievable on your work placement. If you set yourself goals that are unachievable or are unrealistic, you are only likely to get disheartened. So, if you want to make a success of your placement you will need to be realistic in the goals that you set yourself.

What goals do you want to achieve from your work placement? The goals you set could be very simple and straightforward. You may wish to link them to areas you feel you might be able to improve. For example, if you do not have a good record with your timekeeping in school or college then you might want to make "arrive at my placement on time every day" one of your goals. Another way of looking at your goals is to think about what you are good at. You could use the work placement to provide you with proof of this strength. For example, you might say that although timekeeping at school or college was poor, you always arrive on time for your part time job. Your goal could still be "arrive at my placement on time every day". Try to come up with a realistic set of goals for your placement.

Let's Get Going

When he was a small boy, Richard Branson was asked what he wanted to be. He said that he wanted to be a successful businessman. This was probably a realistic goal because he was very focused and he was prepared to work hard to achieve his goal. However, if Richard Branson had said that he wanted to be the owner of a large company like Virgin by the time he was 14 years old, would this have been a realistic goal?

Did you know?

Although David Beckham now seems very confident, he was actually quite shy when he first went to Manchester United. After he got married he became famous not just as a footballer but also as a celebrity. He wasn't used to so much media attention and had to set himself realistic goals on how to handle interviews and how to be photographed. It seems that he has achieved his goals.

Figure 5.8: David Beckham's goal when he was a boy was to play for Manchester United

Activity 12

Have a look at Table 5.3. These set out the goals of four 16 year-olds. Do you think each goal is realistic and achievable? Give your reasons.

Current circumstances	Goal
Working in a supermarket	To be a supermarket manager when I am 30
Working in a hotel	To work hard and get promotion
School leaver with 2 GCSEs	To be a brain surgeon
School leaver with 4 GCSEs	To get a job as a junior office clerk

Table 5.3: The work goals of four young people

PLTS: Reflective learner

When you are thinking about the areas that you need to improve in order to set your work placement goals, you will be practising the skills of a reflective learner.

Functional Skills: Using English

Use your speaking and listening skills to explain how you have chosen your goals with your teacher or tutor and respond constructively to any suggestions.

Case Study

Emily

Emily is going to work in a hotel on her placement. When she has more experience she wants to be a hotel manager. The hotel has offered her a placement in which she will work with its receptionist for two weeks.

Emily has visited the hotel prior to the placement and has discussed her placement with the receptionist. They have agreed on the things that Emily will be doing. Emily has compiled a list of her strengths and the areas where she thinks she needs to improve.

Emily's strengths:

- I learn quickly.
- I get on well with people I don't know.
- I dress well and I think that personal hygiene is very important.

Emily's weaknesses:

- I sometimes fool around and don't behave sensibly.
- I am not confident in unfamiliar situations.
- I can waste time and be easily distracted

Can you suggest some realistic and achievable goals for Emily for her work placement?

Just Checking

* Are your goals realistic?
* Have you talked them through with anybody?

Goal Targets that you want to achieve over time or during a particular activity.

168 Business, Administration and Finance

169

Case study

Case studies show how the concepts covered in this book apply to the real world. Questions and activities will encourage you to push your understanding further.

Just Checking

The most important points to understand, summarised so you can quickly refresh your knowledge.

Key words

Key concepts and new words are explained clearly and simply to make sure you don't miss anything important.

I want to be...
This lets you hear from real people what it is like to work in the Business, Administration and Finance sector.

What you will learn...
Each chapter ends with assessment tips and an opportunity for you to check your skills and summarise what you've learned.

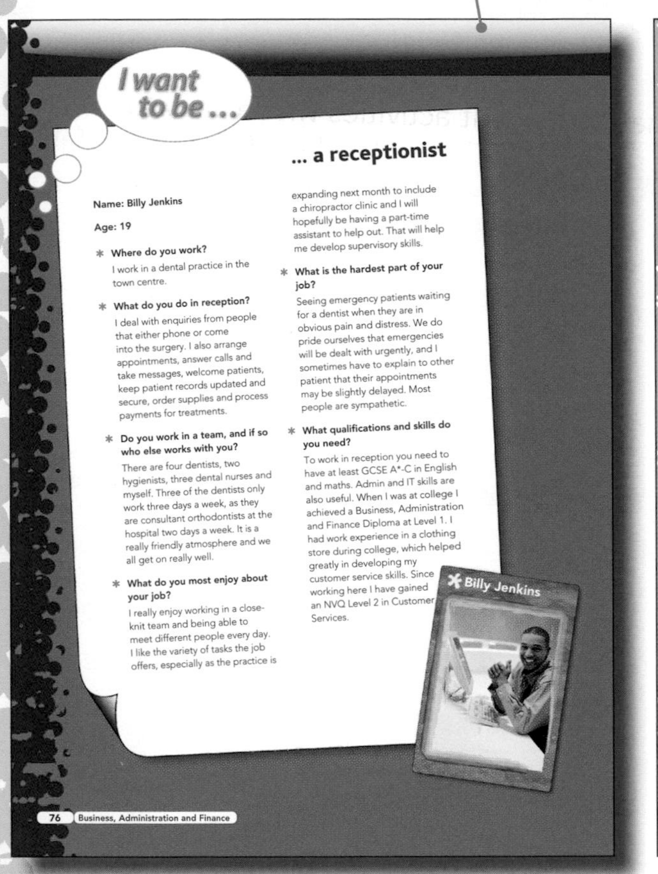

I want to be ...

... a receptionist

Name: Billy Jenkins

Age: 19

* **Where do you work?**
  I work in a dental practice in the town centre.
* **What do you do in reception?**
  I deal with enquiries from people that either phone or come into the surgery. I also arrange appointments, answer calls and take messages, welcome patients, keep patient records updated and secure, order supplies and process payments for treatments.
* **Do you work in a team, and if so who else works with you?**
  There are four dentists, two hygienists, three dental nurses and myself. Three of the dentists only work three days a week, as they are consultant orthodontists at the hospital two days a week. It is a really friendly atmosphere and we all get on really well.
* **What do you most enjoy about your job?**
  I really enjoy working in a close-knit team and being able to meet different people every day. I like the variety of tasks the job offers, especially as the practice is expanding next month to include a chiropractor clinic and I will hopefully be having a part-time assistant to help out. That will help me develop supervisory skills.
* **What is the hardest part of your job?**
  Seeing emergency patients waiting for a dentist when they are in obvious pain and distress. We do pride ourselves that emergencies will be dealt with urgently, and I sometimes have to explain to other patient that their appointments may be slightly delayed. Most people are sympathetic.
* **What qualifications and skills do you need?**
  To work in reception you need to have at least GCSE A*-C in English and maths. Admin and IT skills are also useful. When I was at college I achieved a Business, Administration and Finance Diploma at Level 1. I had work experience in a clothing store during college, which helped greatly in developing my customer service skills. Since working here I have gained an NVQ Level 2 in Customer Services.

Billy Jenkins

76 Business, Administration and Finance

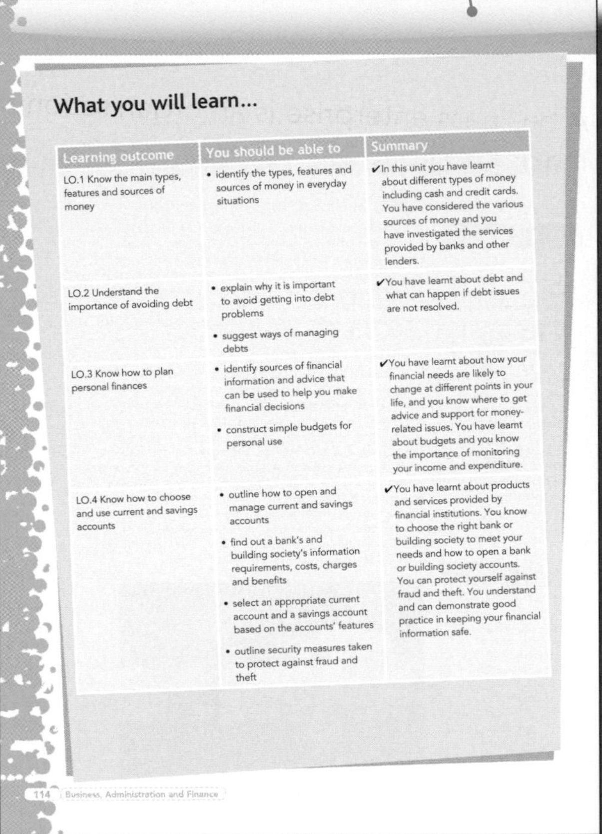

What you will learn...

Learning outcome	You should be able to	Summary
LO.1 Know the main types, features and sources of money	• identify the types, features and sources of money in everyday situations	✔In this unit you have learnt about different types of money including cash and credit cards. You have considered the various sources of money and you have investigated the services provided by banks and other lenders.
LO.2 Understand the importance of avoiding debt	• explain why it is important to avoid getting into debt problems • suggest ways of managing debts	✔You have learnt about debt and what can happen if debt issues are not resolved.
LO.3 Know how to plan personal finances	• identify sources of financial information and advice that can be used to help you make financial decisions • construct simple budgets for personal use	✔You have learnt about how your financial needs are likely to change at different points in your life, and you know where to get advice and support for money-related issues. You have learnt about budgets and you know the importance of monitoring your income and expenditure.
LO.4 Know how to choose and use current and savings accounts	• outline how to open and manage current and savings accounts • find out a bank's and building society's information requirements, costs, charges and benefits • select an appropriate current account and a savings account based on the accounts' features • outline security measures taken to protect against fraud and theft	✔You have learnt about products and services provided by financial institutions. You know to choose the right bank or building society to meet your needs and how to open a bank or building society accounts. You can protect yourself against fraud and theft. You understand and can demonstrate good practice in keeping your financial information safe.

114 Business, Administration and Finance

You can also find help with technical terms in the glossary on p.180.

We hope you enjoy using this book, and we wish you the very best for your Diploma course and your future career in Business, Administration and Finance.

Business Enterprise

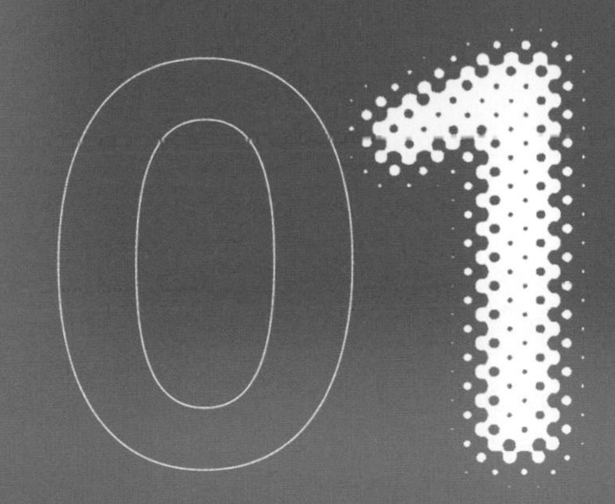

A business enterprise is an organisation that carries out activities with a view to making a profit. Some business enterprises succeed, although others fail. Successful businesses begin with a good idea. All it takes is for someone to identify a new market or a business opportunity and find a way to develop the product or service.

This unit will help you to come up with your own ideas and to identify which are real opportunities for further development. You will investigate a range of business topics such as what makes products and services successful, how to test a market and how to present an idea to people who might invest. You will learn about the things to consider when researching a business idea and how to review its success.

What you will learn in this unit

LO.1 Understand what makes a product or service successful

1.1 Types of product and service

1.2 Keeping up with change

1.3 What makes a product or service successful?

LO.2 Be able to generate and develop an idea for a product or service

1.4 Looking for opportunities and generating ideas

1.5 Deciding which ideas are realistic

LO.3 Be able to test an idea for a product or service

1.6 Market research

1.7 Interpreting market research data

LO.4 Be able to present a business idea

1.8 Presenting your idea

LO.5 Be able to implement and review a business enterprise

1.9 Promotion, estimating demand and setting targets

1.10 Resources and production

1.11 Was the business idea successful?

Assessment

This unit will be assessed by an assignment which will be marked by your teacher or tutor. You will research and develop a business idea, present your idea to potential investors, and implement and review the business idea.

Topic 1.1 Types of product and service

Let's Get Going

Most businesses are categorised by what they do. Some create products that other people or businesses can buy. Others provide a type of service. Write down different:

- Types of product
- Types of service

List as many as you can in each category.

PLTS: Independent enquirer

Completing Activity 1 will demonstrate this skill.

To begin this unit, let's investigate different types of product (items you can buy and touch, like clothes) and different types of service (something that is done for you or to you, like a hair cut). Once you can identify different products and services, you will feel more confident about developing a business idea of your own.

Types of product

Food

Food is a very familiar product. All households need to buy food. Some types of food are grown or produced in the UK. Other foods are imported (brought into this country from overseas). Look at the supermarket shelves and you will find many examples of imported foods.

Activity 1

Next time you visit the supermarket, find five food products that come from somewhere else in the world. These could include manufactured products like biscuits, or grown produce such as fruit and exotic vegetables.

Clothing

Like food, some clothes are manufactured in the UK. However, many items of clothing in UK stores are produced overseas. Some styles have been imported to the UK. Today, a significant proportion of the world's clothing is manufactured in poorer countries where wages are lower than in the UK.

Electrical and electronic goods

Most of today's electrical and electronic products like games consoles, DVDs, MP3 players and digital cameras were developed in countries where significant money has been put into research and development. Many businesses in countries like the United States and Japan invest heavily in new technology.

Activity 2

How many electrical or electronic products do you have in your home? See if you can list 10 different products from at least 3 rooms.

Types of service

Entertainment

A service is something you receive but don't get to keep. For example, you might pay to see a band or to see a film at the cinema. You receive a service (the music, the film), but there is no physical product that you take away after the event.

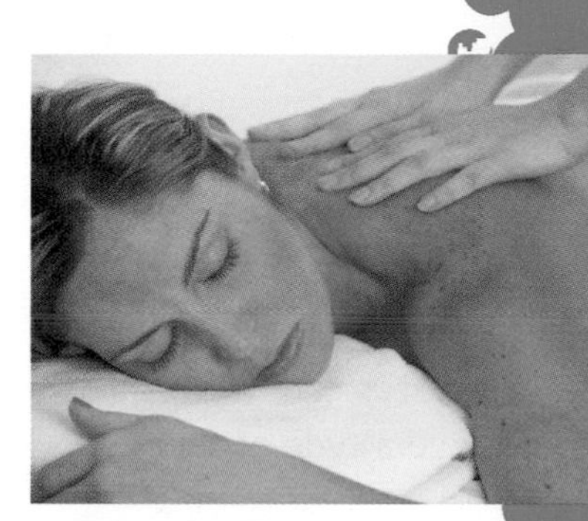

Figure 1.1: Massages are often offered in the beauty industry.

Beauty

The beauty industry is expanding in the UK. It offers many types of service, such as hairdressing, manicures, pedicures and facials. The customer (known in the industry as the client) pays for a specialist to carry out a particular procedure.

Insurance

Insurance is taken out to protect yourself in some way. Table 1.1 lists some of the main types of insurance available.

Insurance	What it's for
Car	To pay (compensate) another person if the insured driver causes an accident or to protect against the driver's car being vandalised or damaged in any way.
Home contents	To protect personal possessions against theft, fire or flood.
Buildings	To protect a building against damage by fire or flood.
Personal life	This insurance will pay out if the person insured dies (although there can be exclusions for some medical conditions).
Holiday	Holiday insurance comes in three parts: it will repay the cost of the trip if it has to be cancelled for genuine reasons; it will cover the loss of possessions during the holiday; and it will cover the cost of any medical treatment required during the trip.

Table 1.1: Main types of insurance

An insurance company sells policies. It receives a payment for each policy. When a policy holder needs to make an insurance claim, this customer informs the insurance company. If the insurance company accepts the claim after investigation, it will make a payment to the customer.

Activity 3

Talk to members of your family. How many different types of insurance do they currently have? Have they had any other policies in the last year, such as holiday insurance?

PLTS: Independent enquirer

When you talk to your family members to identify the different types of insurance they have, you will be showing that you are an Independent enquirer.

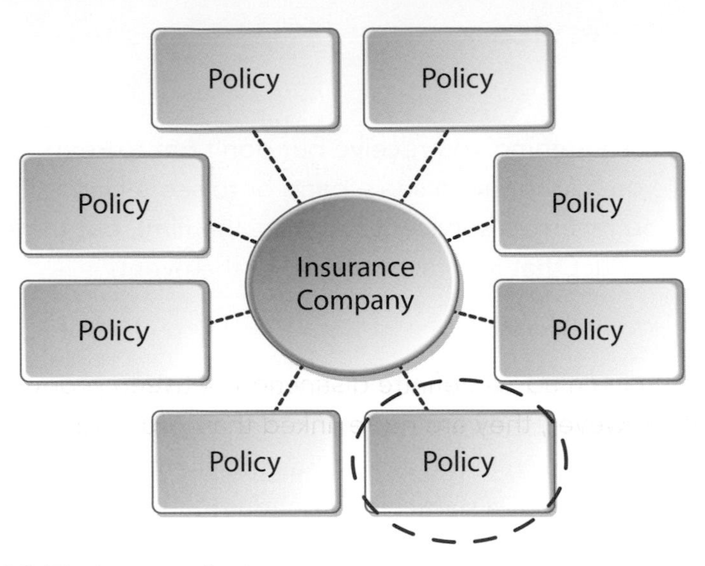

Figure 1.2: The insurance business

To pay claims, an insurance company uses money it has received from selling policies. The assumption is that not all customers will claim on their policies – in other words, the insurance company works on the idea that it will receive more money from the sale of policies than it will pay out through claims. However, some insurance companies have been caught out when there have been major disasters like widespread floods or hurricanes. These natural disasters can result in many customers making claims at exactly the same time.

Note that all insurance policies have restrictions. Make sure that you know what you are buying.

Transport

Taking the train, using a taxi or riding on a bus are all types of service. To repeat the experience you would need to pay for another trip.

Consider the company in which you are based for your work experience placement. Identify whether it makes products or provides services. Note that the company might be involved with both products and services. See what you can find out and make some notes.

Activity 4

After your work placement, use the notes you have made to create a PowerPoint presentation about the company. Set out what it does. Then explain your role within the business and describe the duties you performed.

Links between products and services

So far we have made a definite distinction between products and services. However, they are more linked than you might first think.

Retailing

The retailing industry covers those businesses that sell products directly to the public. Supermarkets, clothes stores and electrical shops are all retailers. Retailers often provide both products and services. For example, many supermarkets also provide services such as a home delivery service and may sell insurance.

Post-sales support

This type of service is often associated with the purchase of electrical goods. Most electrical goods manufacturers will provide a phone number and email address where purchasers can get technical support, or even a website offering advice and guidance on tackling problems. This can be particularly useful when products need to be set up after they have left the store. Note that some companies use the phrase "after-sales service" rather than "post-sales support".

Just Checking

* Describe the difference between a product and a service.
* Give an example of one product type and one service type that hasn't been discussed in this topic.
* Name a business that offers both a product and a service.

PLTS: Reflective learner

Activity 4 will give you an opportunity to demonstrate your skills as a reflective learner.

Functional Skills: Speaking and listening

Presenting to others will enable you to show that you are able to take full part in a formal exchange.

Functional Skills: Using ICT systems

Using PowerPoint will show that you can use ICT systems independently for a particular purpose.

Topic 1.2 Keeping up with change

Let's Get Going

Can you think of three things that have changed about your school or college since you started? If not, talk to your teachers or tutors and see if they can help.

Businesses constantly need to observe and respond to what is going on around them to survive. All companies must make sure that they keep up with changes that might affect their business.

Now consider the different sorts of changes businesses might need to respond to.

Technology

When new technology becomes available, it can often help a business in several ways. For example, businesses can use new technology to make better components that can improve their products. In this way, Microsoft developed the X-Box 360, a more powerful games console that superseded the original X-Box.

When the Nintendo Wii came on the market it was a completely different type of console. This was developed using new infrared technology. The tenpin bowling game, for example, requires the player to swing the wireless, motion-sensitive controller, making a throwing action that is picked up by a sensor.

A business might also use new technology to improve its manufacturing process. This might allow it to produce its existing products more easily, quickly and/or cheaply.

Market needs

Customer needs can change. The best businesses are able to spot gaps in the market – in other words, they can identify products or services that their customers would want but which do not yet exist. Many businesses invest in research and development to try and find new products and services that will appeal to customers.

Fashion

Sometimes businesses respond to fashion. This means that they develop products in response to a particular craze or fad. For example, at the beginning of each year some businesses will try to predict the product that will be the most popular Christmas gift choice for particular social groups, such as young children. They will then steer their activities towards supporting these products, not only directly but also through accessories and connected products. Let's look at an example.

Responding to a new market

Two businesses have heard that a company called Strobilnova Toys is launching a new doll.

Product name: Caroline-Nicole doll

Features: Interchangeable heads, with hair that can be coloured, styled and restyled
Make-up that can be applied, removed and reapplied
MP3 player accessory that can be shared by the doll and the child

Target market: Young girls (6–9 years old)

The two businesses serve different markets. One company makes stationery; the other makes children's clothing. They ask Strobilnova Toys for permission to make some products based around the new doll featuring Strobilnova logos as well as images of the Caroline-Nicole doll. With a partner, consider the different types of clothing or stationery that could be produced to tie in with the launch of the doll. See if you can find five ideas for each company.

PLTS:
Creative thinker

Thinking up possible ideas will show that you are a creative thinker.

The competition

At times businesses have to respond to the activities of their competitors. If a competitor improves an existing product or develops a new product, then a rival business may respond by improving its own product or developing a similar one. Later in this unit when you develop your own business ideas, you will need to identify the competition that exists for your product or service.

To see the effects of competition, consider this example from the cosmetics industry. Traditionally companies developed cosmetic and skin products using chemicals. These products were tested on animals to make sure that they would be safe for people to use. In 1976 Anita Roddick started The Body Shop. The main focus of her stores was to stock vegetable-based products that had not been tested on animals. This proved attractive to customers who agreed with her argument that animal testing was wrong. As The Body Shop products became popular, other cosmetics and skin care companies began to develop similar "natural" product ranges to compete.

Just Checking

* Think of another type of change that businesses might need to respond to.
* Give an example of a service or product that has been developed in response to a particular need.

Topic 1.3 What makes a product or service successful?

Let's Get Going

Let's consider something straightforward – crisps. Do you prefer Walkers crisps or a supermarket's own brand? Why? Perhaps one is cheaper? Or is it the taste? Perhaps you prefer the quality of one type of crisps to the other?

In order to be successful, a product or service needs to have a feature or features that make it desirable. What that desirable feature is may not be the same for all customers. For some people, cost is an important factor. For others, it is functionality. This is one of the reasons why so many businesses spend large amounts of money on market research. Their aim is to discover what it is about particular products and services that makes customers buy them.

Consider universal remote controls. These are single units that can control many different electronic appliances, such as televisions, DVD recorders and satellite boxes. This means that you don't need separate control devices for each appliance. The first businesses that developed these devices had to research whether this would be something that consumers wanted. They had to think about whether they would have wide appeal, and what price people would be prepared to pay.

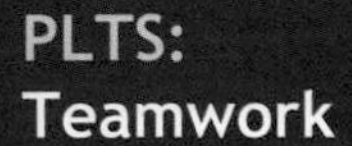

PLTS: Teamwork

Activity 5 will give you an opportunity to show that you can work with other people. In this work you may need to compromise if others in your group have different opinions about the three things that you like about the products and the two things that could be improved.

Functional Skills: Using ICT

Activity 5 will show that you can bring together information and present it in ways that are fit for purpose and audience.

Activity 5

With a group of two or three classmates, choose two of these five products to investigate:

- Nestlé Smarties
- Apple iTunes software
- Nintendo Wii
- Colgate toothpaste
- Wall's Vienetta ice cream

For each of your chosen products describe:

(a) the product

(b) three things you really like about it

(c) two things you think could be improved to make the product even better.

Create two A5 leaflets (one for each product) that present your group's conclusions.

Reasons why a new product or service might be successful

One way of coming up with business ideas that you could investigate and test is to look at adapting or changing existing products and services. Explore ways of changing products and services so that they are different, or ways of making them better or cheaper.

Figure 1.3: The development of the mobile phone

It is different

A product might be successful because it is different from competing products. For example, it might appeal more to customers simply because it is:

- a different colour
- a different shape
- a different size.

It is better

A business might be successful because it makes better products or services than its competitors. It could produce similar products from its rivals but ones which:

- have additional features
- are faster
- are lighter or more stylish.

It is cheaper

Price is important in many markets. Many businesses look for ways to offer cheaper products and services to those currently on offer to customers.

Just Checking

* Consider a product that you (or someone you know) bought recently. Think of two reasons why you chose to buy that particular product rather than the similar ones that were available.
* Products or services can be successful because they are different, better or cheaper than the alternatives. Identify a fourth way in which a product or service might achieve success.

Topic 1.4 Looking for opportunities and generating ideas

Let's Get Going

How many times have you seen the words "new" or "improved" on products that you use? Look in the kitchen cupboards and bathroom cabinets at home and see if you can find products that claim to be either new or improved.

Entrepreneur
Someone who is able to recognise opportunities for new products, services and processes or who can see ways to make improvements to existing products, services and processes. Entrepreneurs need to be creative, brave and prepared to work hard.

Figure 1.4: James Dyson

Have you ever been doing something and suddenly thought "wouldn't life be easier if there was something to do this for me?" This is how many inventions and new ideas are generated, with someone identifying a problem and looking for a way to solve it.

Sometimes new product ideas just happen. Sometimes developers search for them by experimenting with existing products.

People who have the talent to spot new business opportunities are known as entrepreneurs. They have the ability to assemble the resources needed to develop ideas into actual products and services. As important, they can access the finance to pay for the research, development and business start-up costs.

There are two fundamental ways of generating new ideas:

- looking for opportunities
- brainstorming.

Looking for opportunities

Many successful business ventures have been started by an individual **entrepreneur** coming up with a good idea. Some of the UK's most famous entrepreneurs are Sir James Dyson, Sir Alan Sugar and Sir Richard Branson. You may not recognise all of them, but it is likely that you would recognise their products.

James Dyson invented the bagless vacuum cleaner. This product was an improvement on the standard vacuum cleaner because without a bag, it was able to benefit from better power and thus better suction. This meant that as a vacuum cleaner it was more effective than models containing bags.

In the 1980s when computing technology was still very expensive, Alan Sugar recognised before most people that computers could be a hugely successful product. They would not only be used by businesses, but would find their way into people's homes. His business Amstrad (Alan Michael Sugar Trading) developed one of the very first compact and low-cost computer systems for the home market.

Richard Branson, the founder and owner of the Virgin brand, has been involved in many different businesses. His businesses are extremely varied, from Virgin Atlantic, Virgin Trains and Virgin Holidays which provide travel and holidays, to Virgin Earth which funds research to find better solutions to global problems, developing ideas on the better use of energy and ways of lowering emissions.

All good entrepreneurs have something in common: they all have good ideas for products or services and are successful in developing them to be attractive to customers.

Figure 1.5: **Richard Branson**

Brainstorming

Not all companies are owned and operated by far-sighted entrepreneurs. The more common way of generating new ideas is for groups of people within a business to brainstorm. This is where a group of people get together to produce ideas.

The group could aim to develop ideas through discussion or experimentation. Sometimes the group already has a proposal and spends time firing ideas backwards and forwards to improve this proposal until the participants feel that they have a workable product or service. In a brainstorm session all ideas should be recorded, so that time isn't wasted at a later date considering a proposal that has already been discounted.

It goes without saying that the brainstorming approach isn't always successful. It may take many sessions before one good idea is found. However, brainstorming is an approach that you can adopt with friends or classmates. You might start by considering your own interests and skills. Could you develop a hobby into a business idea? Could you use your skills in a new business setting? Have you seen a gap in the market for a particular type of product or service in your local area?

Just Checking

* How do most businesses generate new ideas for products or services?
* What word is used to describe individuals who have a talent for spotting new opportunities?
* Why is it important to record the ideas that are discussed when brainstorming?

Topic 1.5 Deciding which ideas are realistic

Let's Get Going

Businesses must make sure that any idea they want to develop has a chance of becoming successful. To be able to make this decision they need to decide whether the idea is really good. You too will need to make this decision when you develop your own enterprise. To do this, you need to consider three separate areas:

- time, money and available resources
- your knowledge and skills
- the potential market for your product or service idea.

Not every idea is a good one! Have you ever had an idea and then thought sometime afterwards that maybe it hadn't been such a good idea after all? Why do you think that was?

Time, money and resources

You will need to consider whether you have enough time, money and resources to make the business work. In particular, lack of money can be the reason why many really good ideas are sometimes not developed. Even if you have enough time, without sufficient money you will not be able to buy the necessary resources to develop your idea into a product or service that you can sell. So you need to check that your idea is realistic. (In Unit 3 you will learn about different sources of finance.)

Time is another important factor. For example, if you are developing a product or service for the Christmas market, you may already have left it too late if you begin development in, say, September. Will you need to obtain specialist machinery or equipment? Will you be able to obtain any necessary raw materials?

The issue here is not simply availability. It often comes down to finance. Can you afford the things you need? Do you have the money? Insufficient money is the biggest barrier to making a success of the business.

Knowledge and skills

Will you have the skills you need? For example, if you are creating a computer software package, do you have the programming and development skills? Do you know enough about finance to be able to manage the accounts for the business?

You may be able to buy in some of these skills by employing others. However, if you have to pay out for things you should be able to do yourself, you will make less money from the project.

PLTS: Reflective learner

Showing you can reflect on your own skills and knowledge shows that you are a reflective learner.

Activity 6

Think about your own skills and knowledge.

- What three things do you think you know a lot about?
- What three things are you really good at?
- What three things, or in which three areas, do you need to improve?

The potential market

In the next topic you will consider how to test your product in your intended **market**. But first you need to decide whether your product or service idea has a potential market.

Start by thinking back to the different types of products and services you considered at the beginning of this unit. Do you think that there are any limitations or restrictions on how and when particular products could be used or when particular types of service could be delivered? In order to answer this question you need to think about your product in relation to customer needs.

For example, consider a seasonal product such as gloves. These are only usually worn in winter. Customers are likely to buy gloves when the weather starts to get colder. It would not therefore be sensible to introduce a new range of gloves in the spring. Shops are unlikely to want to stock goods that they will find difficult to sell in the summer months.

Activity 7

Identify at least five other products or services for which sales are related to the seasons or are affected by the weather. Use a range of sources including the Internet, magazines and newspapers to come up with ideas. Write notes and place in your portfolio.

Functional Skills: Reading

An activity that requires you to read online and printed material will enable you to show that you can understand a range of texts.

From your research in Activity 7 it should be clear that potential sales for products could be limited depending on the type of product and the particular situations or conditions. For your business enterprise you will need to know if there is a market for your product or service.

Market The target customer group for a product or service. A product might be targeted at children aged 7 to 11, or girls aged 14 to 16, or men in their 30s. These are all examples of markets.

Some businesses pay market research companies to investigate the potential market for their products and services. Sometimes they do this activity themselves. As a result of this research, a business might modify the product or service to meet the needs of the market. In some cases, a planned product launch might be cancelled or an existing product withdrawn from sale.

Businesses have many ways of gathering information that can be used in their market research activities. One method is to use the data captured by store loyalty cards.

Figure 1.6: **Loyalty cards**

What are loyalty cards?

When a store issues a loyalty card to a customer, it records some of the customer's personal details. Each time the customer makes a purchase in the store and presents the card, points are credited on the customer's card. The customer is able to exchange the points for vouchers or free products. The store has a record of the items bought by the customer. It can use this information to draw conclusions about the purchasing patterns of different types of customers.

Functional Skills: Speaking and listening

When you talk to others as part of an investigation this will show that you can take part in informal discussions and exchanges.

Activity 8

Talk to your family and friends. Who has loyalty cards? How many different types of shops issue cards? What sorts of rewards do the customers receive?

Make a list of stores that issue loyalty cards. Record the rewards offered by each store. Make a table of information and print a copy for your portfolio. Make a backup copy of the file and store this in another location or on a storage device (like a USB or CD-ROM).

Functional Skills: Using ICT

When you create tables of information you will be demonstrating that you can select software applications to meet needs, that you can manage information storage and that you can insert and remove an information storage device.

Developing the best idea

Suppose your ideas pass the tests outlined on the previous page. You have decided, for example, that your proposal is realistic as you have sufficient time, money and resources. The next step might be to develop it further by asking yourself these questions.

Who is it for?

You will need to decide who are the likely customers for your product or service. For example, will it appeal to women aged 40 to 50, children under 10, or boys between 12 and 16? The potential customers are known as your target market.

Why do people need it?

You will need to explain why you think the product or service is needed by the target market you have defined. What is its attraction? What benefits will it provide?

The answers to these questions will help you to identify your potential market so you will know who you should test your ideas on. This is important, as you will see in the next topic.

It is a good practice to keep some notes on your product ideas. Figure 1.7 shows a form that you could use to keep a record

Product Idea Form

Name of product		Type of product or service	
Who is it for?		Why do people need it?	

What resources are needed?	Are the resources available?	What knowledge/skill is needed?	Are these available?

Figure 1.7: **Product idea form**

of your product idea. Once you have noted down some basic information about your target market, expand your analysis by recording the types of resources you will need. Note whether these resources are readily available. If they are not readily available, state where you might find them.

Add details on the knowledge and skills you feel are necessary to deliver your product or service. Again state whether these are already available. If not, you might decide to bring in people with the right skills, or you might decide to find a training course so that you can develop these skills yourself.

Once you have a formal outline for your product or service, it is probably a good idea to share this with someone more experienced. This should be a person that you can trust. Some businesses have found that the people they confided in essentially stole their ideas – so trust is essential.

Just Checking

* What are the three important areas to focus on in deciding whether to develop a new idea?
* How can businesses gather market information without directly talking to customers?
* List the two questions you need to answer to help you decide which is the best idea to develop.

Topic 1.6 Market research

Let's Get Going

Have you have ever completed a questionnaire to record your thoughts and feelings about something? Did the questionnaire seek your views on particular products or services? What questions were you asked?

In developing business ideas, it is important to consider who the customers for the proposed product or service are likely to be. These potential customers should be the target group for your market research.

Being able to carry out valid research is a very important skill. It will be useful throughout this course, as well as supporting the development of your business idea in this unit. To test the potential for your product or service, you will need to investigate the market in general, as well as the views of your future customers. Table 1.2 sets out some important considerations.

Area to investigate	Some questions for research
What is the potential competition?	Are there any similar products or services already on the market? If so, how many? What sorts of features and functionality do they have? Are the businesses already trading in this market well known or influential?
What is the size of the target market?	How big is the market for this type of product or service? How many potential customers are in the target market?
What do customers want?	What are customers looking for from the product or service? What features are important? What functionality is important?
What do customers think of your idea?	What do they think of your product or service? What are its good points? What are its bad points? What could be improved?
How much will people be willing to pay?	How much do similar products and services cost? What price range is likely to be attractive to customers?

Table 1.2: Testing the potential of a business idea

All the data you gather as part of your market research will need to be analysed. This will enable you to make sense of your research so that you can make decisions about the features of your product or service. You will cover data analysis in topic 1.7.

The way you carry out your research will depend on your target market. Some research methods are ideal for products and services targeted at business customers, others are better suited for investigating the opinions of individual consumers. Some can be used for any target market.

Market research agents

Figure 1.8: Market research

Some companies specialise in carrying out direct market research for other businesses. Their researchers will find and interview people (or businesses) in the target customer group. Sometimes this is done in a shopping area by simply stopping people as they pass by and recording their answers to some questions. Interviewers are usually given a questionnaire to provide a structure to the process.

Questionnaires

Questionnaires are very useful means of gathering information. They have the advantage of ensuring that each person interviewed answers the same questions.

When you create a questionnaire you need to be really careful how you phrase (or ask) the questions. Questions that are vague may not be correctly understood, and the response might be inappropriate, incorrect or useless.

The questions can have either an open or a closed format.

An open format question will trigger the person being interviewed to give an extended response. Suppose someone is asked: "What sort of food do you like?" This leaves it completely open about how the question should be answered. For example, someone might respond: "Well I like Chinese food. It's really tasty."

A closed format question only allows the person being interviewed to respond with specific answers. Figure 1.9 shows an extract from a customer survey questionnaire. It asks the same question – "What sort of food do you like?" – but limits the possible responses. The questions are closed, because you can only answer yes or no to each option. If the answer for fish is "yes", you tick the box; if the answer is "no", you leave the box blank.

What sorts of food do you like?	Please tick your choices
Meat (such as beef)	
Fish	
Poultry (such as chicken)	
Bread and pasta	
Vegetables	
Desserts	

Figure 1.9: Extract from customer survey questionnaire

Notice that "Chinese and Indian food" is not even an option in the closed format question. If the interviewer used the open question, then the answer from the person who likes Chinese and Indian food would not be in the range (a set of expected values) allowed in the questionnaire.

It is much harder to analyse responses from open questions than from closed questions. Open questions are likely to generate a wide variety of answers, indeed many more than you will expect!

Questionnaires are good for reaching a large number of people. The main disadvantages are that people often complete questionnaires anonymously (so they cannot be identified or contracted again). People may also answer questionnaires untruthfully.

Functional Skills: Using ICT

Choosing the right software to create the required document will show that you can select and use software applications to meet needs and solve given problems.

Activity 9

Create a questionnaire to gather information about people's hobbies and interests. The questionnaire should contain at least five questions about different types of social, sport or leisure activities.

Make sure your questions are written in such a way that you get back the types of responses you want.

Ask ten people in your class or group to complete your questionnaire. Place the completed questionnaires in your portfolio. You will consider the results in activity 11 later in this unit.

Observation

Another way to get information about the target market is to use observation. You can learn about customer behaviour by simply observing people when they are shopping. The researchers are sometimes identified so that shoppers are aware that they are being observed, or they may be hidden from view.

Observation is good at identifying processes that might not be mentioned if you simply asked someone what they did. Like interviews, observation can be very time-consuming. It can also be seen as intrusive. Some people simply do not like being observed and studied in this way. For this reason, this technique should be used with care.

Activity 10

Ask a family member if you can observe them from the moment they get up in the morning to the time they leave the house. You will clearly only be able to do this when it is appropriate for you to do so. Create a list of their activities and actions.

At the end of the same day, ask the person you observed to tell you exactly what they did during the time that they were observed. Check off each item they remember from your list, but don't prompt them.

Did the person remember all activities and actions on your list? If not, write down why you think that specific activities and actions might have been forgotten. Place in your portfolio and discuss with your teacher/tutor.

PLTS: Independent enquirer and reflective learner

Activity 10 will provide evidence that you can work as an independent enquirer when you carry out your observations.

It will also show that you are a reflective learner if you can explain why the person you observed forgot particular information about their activities.

Interviews

Interviews can be very useful for gathering a variety of information. A structured interview is planned in advance. It is based on a series of prepared questions or points for discussion. An unstructured interview is less well planned and uses many more open questions.

The advantage of using interviews for market research is that this allows the interviewer to explore an area more fully by asking further questions should a really interesting issue present itself. The disadvantage of this technique is that it is time-consuming to carry out each interview.

Focus groups

Another successful method of research is to sit with a group of potential customers to discuss a particular product or service. The individuals who take part in focus groups are usually carefully selected, based on common characteristics like age and gender or because they share particular attitudes, likes or dislikes.

Figure 1.10: Focus groups are a useful research method

Just Checking

* List three different ways of doing market research.
* Why are questionnaires widely used?
* What is the disadvantage of using observations or interviews as a research method?

Topic 1.7 Interpreting market research data

By using questionnaires, observations and focus groups, businesses can obtain a large amount of information on a target market. This needs to be analysed. You will need to be able to interpret (make sense of) your market research. Let's look at an example of how this can be done.

Let's Get Going

Market research data is of little use until it has been analysed. Imagine, for example, that your class is choosing where to go on a school trip. Conduct some market research within your class, giving the class 3 options of where to go, and produce a pie chart of your results.

Functional Skills: Mathematics

This topic will show that you can collect and record discrete data and organise and represent information in different ways.

Interpreting data

A company wants to launch a new mobile phone. As part of its research, the company has arranged for a group of 100 boys and 100 girls to be interviewed. Each individual was asked to pick the feature they think is most important on a mobile phone from a list:

	Boys	Girls	Total
MP3 player	21	17	38
Internet connectivity	7	4	11
Address book	16	12	28
Camera	12	19	31
Bluetooth	14	16	30
Infrared	13	11	24
Video	8	6	14
Games	9	15	24

Table 1.3: Most important mobile phone features

Table 1.3 shows the results of this survey. Use the data in the total column to produce a column chart. Is it easier to see the most popular feature in the table or the column chart?

But what if the company wanted to target a phone at the female market? The data shows that girls have a different set of preferences from the group as a whole.

Of course the company will not be able to please everyone, but it might aim to please as many potential customers as possible. Figure 1.11 offers a further view of the data. From this chart, we can get a really good feel for customer preference because we can compare the choices of boys and girls. Here are some conclusions.

- MP3 players are a popular feature, although it is more important to boys than girls.
- Girls prefer to have a camera as a feature.
- Neither boys nor girls are particularly concerned about Internet connectivity or video functionality.

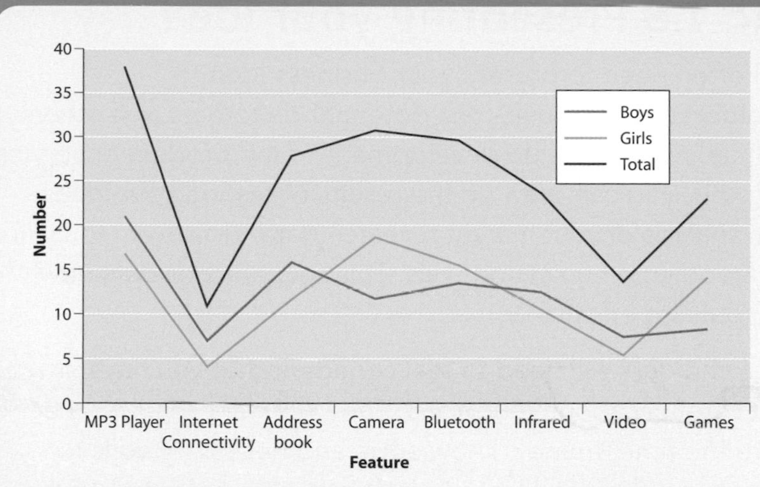

Figure 1.11: Comparing the preferences of boys and girls

These results will help the company to decide which features to include in its products and whether to launch two phones targeted separately at boys and girls.

If you conduct market research on your business idea and undertake similar analysis, you might decide to change some of the features of your planned product or service. You might also realise that you have to include some new ones!

Activity 11

Analyse the results of the questionnaire survey you undertook in activity 9. Draw conclusions about the most popular hobbies, interests and activities of your fellow learners. Create a short PowerPoint presentation to present the results to a group of your colleagues.

PLTS: Independent enquirer and creative thinker

The activity will provide evidence that you are an independent enquirer and a creative thinker as you make sense of the results and draw conclusions.

Just Checking

* Why is it important to understand the results of research?
* What does organising results by "order of preference" tell you?
* Why are charts and graphs better at representing the results of market research than tables of numbers?

Functional Skills: Mathematics

Analysing your own research demonstrates that you can extract and interpret information.

Topic 1.8 Presenting your idea

Let's Get Going

Persuading investors is not always an easy task. Think about occasions when you have asked other people for money.

You will often need to present your business idea to **stakeholders**, such as investors, potential customers and others who will be involved in the development of the product or service. In doing this, you can draw on the results of testing your ideas and any analysis of your market research data. However, you will require good communication skills. This section considers how you can present effectively.

Stakeholder An individual or group of people who have an interest in a particular business or organisation. A company's stakeholders include its customers, suppliers, shareholders, investors, employees and the local community.

Your stakeholders will need to feel confident that you have thought carefully about your plans. They will want to know that you have the time, money, knowledge and necessary skills to see the project through. They do not, however, need to know absolutely everything about what you have done.

Have you ever seen the BBC television programme *Dragons' Den*? In this programme people present their ideas for products and services and try to persuade successful business people to invest in their businesses. If you have the opportunity to see an episode, look at how people make their presentations to the dragons. (You can access the programme's homepage at www.bbc.co.uk/dragonsden.)

How do you impress potential investors with your business idea?

First, think about how to order your information. This is a good plan.

(a) Begin by explaining what you are trying to achieve.

(b) Explain your product or service.

(c) Describe how you researched the market.

(d) Present results of your market research and outline the conclusions that you have drawn.

(e) Explain how many of the product or service you think you will be able to sell.

(f) Talk about how much profit you expect to make.

(g) Explain why you think the idea is a good one.

Presentation

Whether you find yourself presenting to one or two people or to a much larger group, your presentation should be professional. You should create a PowerPoint presentation to give your audience something to look at, and support your talk with handouts where appropriate.

Figure 1.12: Using an interactive whiteboard for presentation

How to be positive and identify benefits

Using the right vocabulary in your presentation is essential. You should use positive words and avoid negative ones.

You will need to identify and share with your audience all the benefits of the product or service. Avoiding negative words will make your audience feel much more confident about your ideas.

Positive words	Negative words
Good	Bad
Right	Wrong
Excellent	Poor
Absolutely	Absent
Effective	Missing
Fabulous	Awful
Distinctive	Unpleasant
Recommended	Dangerous
Rewarding	
Safe	

Table 1.4: Some common positive and negative words

Hotlink

Many more positive words can be found at:

www.winspiration.co.uk/positive.htm

Thinking point

How often are you given handouts in class? What do you do with the handouts? Will you be able to find them if you need to refer to them again?

PLTS: Reflective learner

Thinking about your handouts and how you use them is an example of your skills as a reflective learner.

Anticipating questions you may be asked

You should think carefully beforehand about the sorts of questions you might be asked by your audience. Try as far as possible to anticipate what they might ask, and prepare your answers.

Use of supporting materials

If you have prepared a PowerPoint presentation, you could print out copies of your slides as handouts. Try to organise the handouts, so that you get more than one slide to the page. You can select this option when you go to print the document. You could also create other handouts containing additional information. This could include information that you may not wish to include in the slide show but you feel that your audience should have.

Communicating well

The way you communicate in your presentation says much about your professionalism. In particular, you should aim to create a good impression through the way you speak (your use of voice) and your body language, and by making frequent eye contact with your audience. Here are some simple pointers.

Use of voice

You should be careful to speak at the right speed. Your audience will become bored if you speak too slowly. However, they will not be able to keep up with you, or may not understand what you are saying, if you speak too quickly.

Practising beforehand will allow you to time how long it takes to deliver your talk. Time your presentation and adjust your speaking speed to get closer to the time you are allowed. Good presentations have usually been carefully planned and practised at least three times.

Choose your words carefully. You should aim for clarity and be careful to use appropriate terminology.

Body language

Your body language is important. Positive body language includes smiling, standing confidently and not fidgeting. You should not fold your arms as this can be seen as a barrier between you and the audience.

Figure 1.13: Professionally dressed

Choose your clothes carefully. Dress smartly. Do not wear jeans, T-shirts or trainers, as this will not give the right impression.

Activity 12

Ask a classmate to observe you practising and to give you feedback on your body language. Discuss this with your teacher or tutor.

PLTS: Reflective learner

Thinking about your body language will show your skills as a reflective learner.

Eye contact

Make eye contact with your audience as you speak. This means looking around the room and actually looking directly at as many of the audience as you can. This is something that comes easier with experience and many people find it really difficult to do when they first give presentations.

Try using this trick. Find the person who is furthest to the left in the audience and the person who is furthest to the right. Draw an imaginary line over the top of their heads (see Figure 1.14). When you look towards the audience, don't look directly at any particular person but look over the tops of their heads along your imaginary line. In most cases, the audience will not realise that you are not looking directly at them! It can make a real difference, particularly if you are nervous.

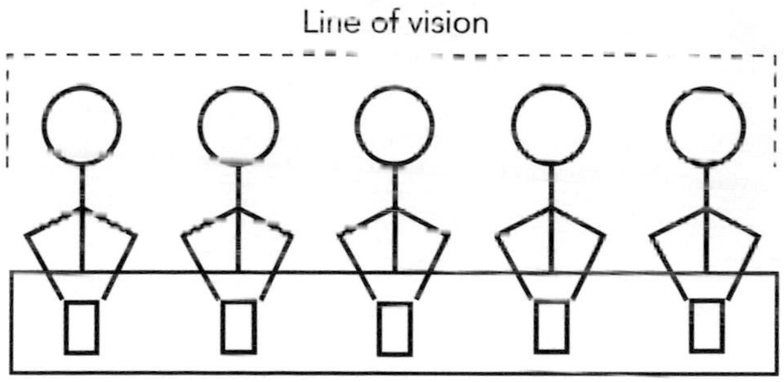

Line of vision

Figure 1.14: **Making eye contact**

If you are able to make eye contact, you will come across as much more confident than someone who constantly looks at their notes or at the presentation on the screen.

Just Checking

* List five things you can do to impress potential investors.

Topic 1.9 Promotion, estimating demand and setting targets

Let's Get Going

Have you ever read through advertisements when you wanted to buy something? How many different places did you need to look before you found what you were looking for?

Once you have decided on your product or service, explored your target market and recruited workers and investors, the implementation process can begin.

Promotion methods

Promotional material is designed to attract the attention and interest of potential customers in products or services.

Advertisements

Advertising can be found in newspapers, magazines and on some television and radio stations. Adverts should always be as short and informative as possible. Images can also be powerful but any picture must be relevant to the content of the advert.

Advertising

Figures 1.15 and 1.16 show advertisements for a cat boarding service. Both versions have exactly the same text. Which version do you think is more effective? Give your reasons.

Cat Boarding Service
Going on holiday? Give your cat a holiday too.

Let us look after your cat.
Vacancies for Summer 09.
Competitive rates.

Call Josie on 05555 555555

Figure 1.15: **Version 1**

Cat Boarding Service
Going on holiday? Give your cat a holiday too.

Let us look after your cat.
Vacancies for Summer 09.
Competitive rates.

Call Josie on 05555 555555

Figure 1.16: **Version 2**

Leaflets or flyers

Leaflets or flyers can be a cheap method of advertising. These can be easily distributed through letterboxes, or by handing them to passers-by, or by placing under the windscreen wipers of cars.

Posters and notices

Posters and notices are often put up in places where people are likely to see them. The content of a poster or notice is usually similar to that used in advertisements, but the actual style will depend on the audience the business is trying to attract.

Activity 13

On your way home from school or college, see if you can find three posters or notices on public display. Write down what they are for and where you saw them (take digital photographs where you can).

Use the information and photos to create a leaflet with the title: "Posters and notices on my route home".

Demonstrations

Demonstrations are a popular way of introducing new products and services because potential customers can see how they work before buying. Often the features of electrical appliances and gadgets, or how to prepare foods will be demonstrated in shops. You may also see people demonstrating services such as massages.

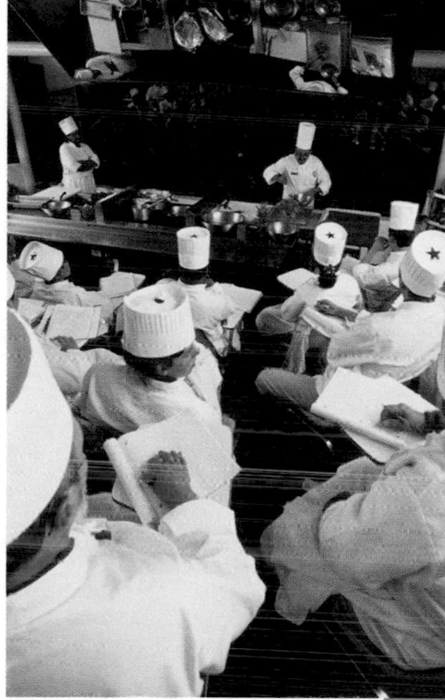

Figure 1.17: Demonstrating cookery techniques

Starting the implementation process

Now that you have thought about the promotion of your product, you will need to organise the people who will help you. You may need to have people involved in sales, accounts and purchasing, and also production and distribution for a product.

You should choose individuals to take these roles carefully. Take into account their personal skills.

Estimating demand and setting sales targets

In order to make sure that you make enough of your product or you provide enough opportunities for customers to use your service, you will need to estimate your likely actual sales.

You will do this using your research to set sales targets. You should try to ensure that your sales targets will be sufficient to allow you to **break even**.

Break even In sales, if you receive enough money to cover your actual costs this is when you break even.

Meeting sales targets will be one of the main ways in which you can assess whether your business idea has been successful.

Just Checking

* Think about which role you would take in the implementation process. Why do you think it would be appropriate for you?
* Identify the role you think you would be least likely to take in the implementation process.

Topic 1.10 Resources and production

To give your idea a chance of success, you need to carefully consider how you acquire your resources and how you will make your product or deliver your service.

Your business is likely to be very small initially. If you are making a product, then your production line is likely to be very small scale. If you are providing a service, you will probably carry out one process or treatment at a time. However, in both instances, you will still need to consider some resource issues.

Let's Get Going

When you are making something, where do you source the raw materials? If you need to buy them, where can you do this? What helps you to make your decisions?

How do you select suppliers?

It is essential to get the best deal you can for any materials and equipment that you will need to make your product or carry out your service. As your costs increase, your profits will get lower. Try to find the best prices you can.

How much will you need?

Once you have found the best supplier, you will need to decide how many (or how much) you will need to buy. It is usually best not to buy too many raw materials when you first start in case your sales are lower then you anticipate. Estimate your sales for say a month, and buy enough materials to make that number of products (or deliver that amount of service).

How will you set the prices?

You should have tried to establish how much customers would pay for your product or service in your market research. The key is not to set your prices so high that people just won't buy, but not to make it so low that potential customers will doubt your product's quality. Try and make sure that your prices are in the same range as your competitors.

When you start out in business, your costs are likely to be relatively high. You will need to make sure that your costs, including the labour costs, are covered. However, do not set prices too high, because as your business develops you will be able to reduce your costs. For example, you will probably be able to get better deals on your materials once you start making repeat orders. Your earnings may be small when you begin, but your profits should increase if the business is successful.

How will you produce the product or service?

Until you know that your business is going to be successful, you will not really want to buy property or expensive machinery or equipment. If you need premises, you could at first try to rent property on a short term let. This is where you only rent the property for a few weeks or months. You could also try to rent machinery and equipment rather than buy it.

Figure 1.18: Large manufacturing machines can be rented

How important is monitoring?

When making a product it is important that the production process is carefully monitored. You need to make sure that each item is produced to a good quality. This might mean that you will need to slow down the production process to avoid errors. Quality is usually better than quantity. It will be more cost effective to produce slightly fewer items to a higher quality, so that fewer products are rejected and wasted.

Quality is not the only consideration. It is important to monitor the process itself. Check that there is as little wastage as possible.

Just Checking

* Where do you get your school clothes from?
* Are you limited to a single supplier or can you buy from different places?
* Why is it important to monitor production quality?

Topic 1.11 Was the business idea successful?

You will need to carry out an evaluation so that you can assess whether your business idea has been a success. Your market research results can provide some criteria that you could use to measure whether the business is a success.

Let's Get Going

Have you ever been asked to evaluate something that you have made? Why do you think reflection or evaluation is important? What can you learn from the process?

Evaluation

When planning your business idea, you may have set some targets that you wanted to achieve. For example, in section 1.9 it was suggested that you set sales targets. You may also have set a target for how much profit you would make. A good place to start your evaluation is to measure the actual business performance against these indicators or targets.

Success should not be measured solely on meeting targets. You could also ask your customers to give their views on your product or service. Were they pleased with what they received? In addition, you might like to ask the people who helped you with the business to give you feedback on how they thought it went.

Figure 1.19: Balancing positive and negative aspects of the business idea

The indicators of success

The main indicators of success for any business are the sales and profit figures. You will need to say whether you achieved your sales targets or made fewer sales than you originally estimated. Similarly, you will need to be able to say whether you made the profit you anticipated.

You will also be expected to identify the decisions that worked particularly well. For example, you might have chosen the right suppliers and got a good deal on your raw materials. You might have pitched (set) the price accurately for the market in which you were competing. Explain what went well, and why. Similarly, explain what didn't work out so well.

The final part of an evaluation is to say what you might do differently next time. This is where you show that you understand any mistakes you made. Explain how you might avoid similar mistakes if you went through the whole process again.

It is useful to record your thoughts in an evaluation document. Draw up and fill in a form like the one in Figure 1.20.

Business Idea Evaluation

Name of Business..
Type of Business ....

Expected sales		Actual sales	
Expected profit		Actual profit	

What went well?	Why?
What went badly?	Why?
How could you improve next time? Give two ways.	

Figure 1.20: Evaluation form

In addition to evaluating the success of your business idea yourself, you should also ask other people for their views.

What about the people who helped you to implement the idea and deliver the product or service?

- Do they think the business idea has been successful?
- Did they enjoy being part of the process?
- What do they think you might have done differently?

What about your customers? Do they feel there are any further improvements that could have been made to the product or service?

What about anybody that invested money in your business? Do they believe that the business has proved to be a successful investment?

It is important to learn not only from your own evaluation of your performance, but also from feedback from others.

Just Checking

* Why is evaluation important?
* What can you learn from evaluation?
* List at least two others whom you could get involved in the evaluation process.

For many years your local community has entered the Britain in Bloom competition. The committee has just discovered that this year it has won a prize. This is likely to attract many more tourists to the area. The committee sees this as an opportunity to raise money for next year's competition.

The idea is to provide something for these tourists to buy when they visit. This could include products such as souvenirs as well as services such as tours of the town.

The committee has asked you to be part of the team that will decide on these new products and services. You should try to make sure that there will be something of interest to different types of visitors, including older people, families (including something for younger children) and horticultural enthusiasts.

You will need to work in a group to make these decisions, as this would be a daunting project for anyone to undertake alone.

Tasks

With three of your classmates complete these tasks:

1 Use a brainstorming approach to generate ideas for products and services that you think might be appropriate for the extra visitors to your area.

  Write down at least three products and two services that you think might meet the committee's requirements. (You can make a bigger list and narrow down your choices later.)

2 As a group you will need to agree on one product or service to develop. Write a short paragraph that describes the product or service that you have chosen. Briefly explain why you think it will be successful.

3 Collect market research data by creating a questionnaire to ask others what they think of your idea. Use this as an opportunity to establish:

  (a) what features the product or service should have

Figure 1.21: Britain in Bloom

(b) how much potential customers would be prepared to pay for the product or service.

4 Use your questionnaire for market research. Obtain completed questionnaires from at least 10 people. Then analyse and interpret the results.

5 Use the results of your analysis to decide on the features of your product or service.

6 Identify the resources you will need to make your product or provide your service. Try to find out where you will be able to source these resources (you might need to talk to your teacher/tutor for ideas).

7 Work out how much it will cost you to make the product or deliver the service. You will need to take into account the resources you will need. Use this information and the results of your market research to set a price.

8 Decide how you will advertise and promote the product or service.

9 Decide how you would organise people working on the project if your idea is implemented.

10 Create a PowerPoint presentation to explain your business idea to the committee. Present all your work and findings. You will need to convince the committee to provide the finance to implement the business idea. So you will need to make a persuasive case for investing in your business idea.

11 Deliver your presentation to your teacher or tutor.

PLTS: Various

Undertaking the case study activity will contribute to these personal learning and thinking skills:

- independent enquirers
- creative thinkers
- team workers
- self-managers
- effective participators.

Functional Skills: Speaking and listening

Working together to plan and execute a project will show that you can make relevant contributions to discussions, responding appropriately to others. It should also allow you to demonstrate that you are flexible in discussions, making different kinds of contributions. Presenting your work will show that you are able to communicate in a formal setting.

Functional Skills: Writing

Checking your work for spelling and grammar will demonstrate your developed skill in this area.

I want to be ...

... an entrepreneur

Name: Luka Dansha

Age: 26

* **How did you become an entrepreneur?**

I had always been really interested in business and at school I got involved in all sorts of money-making schemes, including raising money for charity. I found that I had a real gift for persuading people to invest in good ideas. I continued to think of lots of schemes after school and now it has paid off – I own a number of successful businesses.

* **What sort of training did you have?**

I completed a Business, Administration and Finance course and then went to work for a marketing company. This was very important as it taught me the basics of advertising and product marketing.

* **What sort of skills do you need to be an entrepreneur?**

You need to be able to do more or less anything that the business needs, because you might not always have staff to help you. You must be flexible and willing to do whatever it takes, including working long hours.

* **How do you find the finance to support the development of your business ideas?**

I use a range of organisations to help me, such as banks and building societies as well as business organisations like Business Link.

* **Are there any downsides to being an entrepreneur?**

I think there are probably downsides to any career. I think the main problem with being an entrepreneur is the risk – there is always a chance that the idea can fail. That said, if you do have a good product and do research properly this does minimise the risk.

* **Do you still enjoy being an entrepreneur?**

Yes, it's brilliant! Every week brings a new challenge so I'm constantly learning, which is great. I don't think I could ever go back to working for someone else.

This unit will be assessed by an assignment connected to running a business enterprise. The assignment will be marked by your teacher or tutor.

You will be required to:

- decide on an idea for a product or service and carry out research to test the idea:
  - a list of the ideas you thought of; a description of the idea you chose and why
  - background research into an existing product or service: a description of what it is, who the main market is, why it has been successful
  - the market research carried out to test your chosen idea: method(s) used; key findings; how you used the results to modify the idea
- present the idea to potential investors: what the idea is and why it is worth investing in
- put the business idea into practice and then write up: what decisions were taken and why, and how successful the business was.

To pass this assignment you will give information about different types of products or services and you will show that you understand some of the reasons why products and services are successful. You will also show that you have explored business ideas and will explain the reasons why a particular idea has been chosen for development. Higher marks will be awarded if your explanations are clear and you show you have considered a range of factors in your decision.

When testing your idea and presenting it to potential investors, higher marks will be given if testing is shown to be more rigorous and you show that your interpretation of results has had a direct influence on the business idea if adaptation has been necessary. You will show confidence in the presentation of your idea.

You will work in a group to implement the business idea so you must show that you can work with others to achieve set goals, and that you can be a reliable and committed team member who can demonstrate perseverance even if things do not always go to plan.

When reviewing the business idea and assessing how successful the idea has really been, explain how the results achieved compared with the planned and expected outcomes at the beginning of development. Providing good supporting evidence will enable you to achieve higher marks.

What you have learned in this unit...

Learning outcome	What you have learned	You should be able to
LO.1 Understand what makes a product or service successful	In this unit you have considered a range of products and services and have developed an understanding of why some business ideas are successful.	✔ describe a product or service ✔ explain what makes it successful
LO.2 Be able to generate and develop an idea for a product or service	You have explored how to generate ideas for products and services and investigated how to judge which ideas are realistic and should be developed.	✔ generate ideas for a product or service, reaching agreement to select a workable idea for development
LO.3 Be able to test an idea for a product or service	You have learned how to carry out market research and the different methods you can use for this activity. You have also learned how to use the results of market research to provide information that can be used to help make business decisions.	✔ collect market research data ✔ interpret market research data
LO.4 Be able to present a business idea	You have improved your communication skills and have learned how to prepare, give and support a presentation.	✔ communicate a business idea to an audience ✔ present a persuasive case for investing in a business idea
LO.5 Be able to implement and review a business enterprise	You have learned about teamwork and how to work with others to achieve an end result. You will understand why it is important to show commitment. You will also understand how activities are reviewed by comparing actual results against targets and plans.	✔ collaborate with others and work towards the goal of implementing a business idea, showing commitment and perseverance ✔ take decisions when implementing a business idea ✔ assess how successful the business idea has been

Business Administration, Teams and Communication

In today's marketplace all businesses need effective and efficient administration to support their everyday activities. In this unit you will find out how business administration contributes to the success of any organisation. You will investigate the activities carried out to support different administrative functions.

You will learn how to produce simple business documents using standard office equipment. You will develop the skills and knowledge to be a useful employee and carry out interesting and challenging administrative tasks such as reception duties. Finally, you will learn the importance of communications and teamwork.

Most jobs, even at senior level, require some administrative skills. So learning about, and developing, these skills will provide a firm foundation for success in the workplace.

What you will learn in this unit

LO.1 Know administrative processes used in businesses

2.1 What is administration?

2.2 Administrative processes

LO.2 Be able to produce simple business documents

2.3 What are business communications?

2.4 Business letters

2.5 Other written business communications

2.6 Managing information

LO.3 Be able to plan and carry out administrative work safely

2.7 Planning work

2.8 Using office equipment safely

LO.4 Be able to work as part of a team

2.9 What is a team?

2.10 What makes an effective team?

Assessment

This unit will be assessed by a single assignment that will involve working in a team to plan and produce written communication for a business.

Topic 2.1 What is administration?

Let's Get Going

Think about the different types of administrative jobs that you would like to do. Working in small groups, discuss what activities you think happen in an office.

In business, administration is the activities necessary to support the main operations such as production, sales and marketing. This involves tasks such as dealing with information, handling mail, answering customer queries and producing business documents.

Many people start their careers in administrative roles. There are many different jobs you can do in administration, including administrative assistant, receptionist, personnel assistant and invoice clerk.

Administrative job roles

Functional area This is a specific business function, such as customer services, human resources and production. A functional area could be the responsibility of an individual, a section or a department.

Organisations need administration to help them run effectively. This is true for all organisations, regardless of the nature of their business or their role in the economy. To understand this, let's consider the three main sectors of the economy.

- **Private sector** – Comprises all businesses, large and small, owned and run by private individuals (or groups of individuals). It includes a one-person mobile hairdressing business, which would involve administrative activities such as maintaining client records and major supermarkets like Tesco, with a whole range of administrative job roles such as customer service and human resources.
- **Public sector** – Organisations owned and run by central and local government, including the National Health Service and schools. Typical administrative activities include organising and supporting meetings, filing records and providing performance-related information.
- **Voluntary sector** – This sector includes all charities. Many charity staff are volunteers working for nothing, but some are paid professionals, especially management. Administrative job roles would include managing donations.

Although organisations in the private, public and voluntary sectors have different broad aims, every organisation needs administrative support if it is to meet its objectives.

Activity 1

Working in small groups, research at least two organisations from each sector. From your research, identify three different types of administrative job roles in each organisation. Make a wall chart of your findings.

Business functions

Table 2.1 sets out the main functional areas of a business. A manufacturing business will have a production department. A service organisation will have an operations team to deliver services to its customers and clients.

In a large organisation, each **functional area** might be in a separate department. The departments need to work together to make the business work efficiently. In a small business, one person (or one small team) might undertake several functions.

Business function	Activities
Human resources	Recruitment, training, wages and involvement in industrial relations
Sales and marketing	Carry out market research, market analysis, develop a marketing strategy
Finance	Record income and expenditure, check and pay invoices, prepare the payroll
Administration and IT	Reception, mail, accommodation, maintenance, cleaning, security
Customer services	Deal with customer enquiries and problems about products and services, provide after-sales service, review customer feedback to improve service
Distribution	Prepare delivery documentation and ensure deliveries match orders, plan vehicle routes and deal with any distribution problems
Production	Purchase parts and materials, control production process, monitor budgets and quality of product, maintain production schedule
Operations	Deliver services to customers, manage staff providing frontline services

Table 2.1: Business functions

Find out the different administrative activities undertaken in the key functional areas of the business in which you are doing your work placement.

Just Checking

* Identify two administrative job roles in organisations in each of the three main sectors of the economy.
* Name four business functions which require administrative support.
* List the main activities of these business functions.

Functional Skills: Using English

You will demonstrate speaking and listening skills in contributing to group discussions. You will need to record your findings in writing, so make sure you write clearly and coherently, presenting information in a logical sequence.

Topic 2.2 Administrative processes

Let's Get Going

Think about the administrative skills needed by a receptionist employed in a busy hotel, and those needed by an invoice clerk in a finance department. Working in small groups, discuss the different skills required in each job.

Now that you have considered the main business functions within organisations, you should be able to see there is a huge range of administrative jobs. These jobs often require specific skills and abilities but involve similar types of tasks and processes. In this topic you will examine common administrative processes.

Administrative jobs can be fun and challenging. In some jobs you work in a team; in others you will work on your own. Although the responsibilities will differ with each job role, you should be prepared to undertake any of the tasks discussed here.

Using telephone systems

You should be able to make, receive and transfer calls. All should be done in a courteous and professional manner as you are representing your organisation.

Most organisations have standards for answering the telephone. Some have a standard message to answer with, such as: "Good morning, this is ABC Systems. How may I help you?" Some organisations require that calls are answered within a certain number of rings. It is important to take accurate messages and pass them to the right colleague. Record the caller's name, their requirements and message, and check the message back with the caller.

When making calls you should know the purpose of the call, who to contact and what information you are getting across.

Dealing with visitors

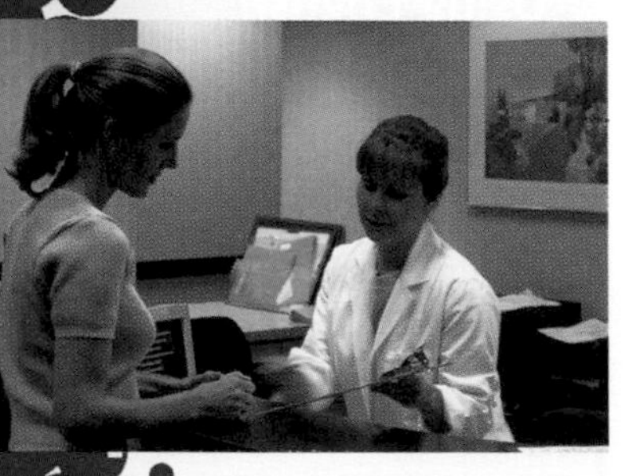

Figure 2.1: A receptionist dealing with a visitor

Employees must create the right image when welcoming visitors to the organisation. Companies will want to create a positive first impression by providing a safe and tidy reception area, and will expect staff to adhere to any dress code. You should welcome visitors by smiling and making eye contact, finding out the purpose of their visit, and then dealing with them according to the organisation's procedures. For example, you might ask them to sign in, issue a name badge, advise the appropriate people that their visitor has arrived, and direct the visitor to the right room. It is important therefore to know the organisation's structure and be familiar with any organisation chart.

Some visitors may have specific requirements. For example, if a visitor has a hearing difficulty, speak slowly and clearly, and face the visitor as facial expressions and gestures help their understanding.

In our multicultural society you will come into contact with many customers for whom English is not their first language. Some may not speak English at all. One way to communicate with visitors who have little English is to write down the message you wish to get over. Sometimes it is easier for a non-English speaking person to understand the written language as they can look up the words they don't understand in a dictionary.

Activity 2

When you visit different organisations, either as part of your course or in your own time, note how you are welcomed on arrival. Are you given a warm, friendly welcome? How does the welcome make you feel? Does the welcome present a positive image? What could be done differently to improve the service to visitors?

Dealing with enquiries

Administrative staff are often required to provide information to internal and external customers, both in writing and orally. You need good communication skills to give accurate and up-to-date information. You also need to be careful to respect any security and confidentiality issues when giving information.

Managing filing systems

Most organisations use a combination of manual and electronic filing systems. It is important to know how to use these systems to store and update records. Records must be easy to access, but security and confidentiality must be maintained.

Most organisations have their own procedures on how and where to store documents. Here are three common ways of organising manual filing systems:

- **alphabetic**, arranging files in alphabetical order
- **numerical**, providing each file with a unique number and compiling an index card so that you can quickly check the contents
- **chronological**, organising files in date order.

Electronic filing systems are increasingly popular because they allow files to be retrieved quickly. They take up much less space than paper systems, provide speed of access and, with appropriate back-up, make it much more difficult to lose documents.

An effective filing system should be easy to use. What systems are used in the organisation in which you are doing your work placement? How effective are they? How easy are they to use?

Figure 2.2: A mailroom

- **Agenda** A list of the topics to be discussed at a meeting, setting out the order in which they will be covered.

Minutes A written record of a meeting. They list the names of people attending, summarise the discussions and any decisions taken, and set out anything that needs to be done following the meeting.

Handling mail

Every organisation will have a procedure for dealing with incoming and outgoing mail. This will usually set out how mail should be sorted, distributed and collected.

A typical procedure for receiving mail would be to sort according to urgency. Special deliveries, which are signed for, would be given priority. If the mail is to be opened and recorded, it is usually date stamped and checked for enclosures before delivering to recipients. You should check with a supervisor how to deal with damaged items or suspicious packages.

For outgoing mail, the process would usually be to check that all letters are addressed and sealed, and parcels are correctly packaged. The weight and size of letters and parcels must be checked prior to stamping or franking. All post would then be prepared for collection by the postal service provider or taken to the provider's depot.

Activity 3

Investigate different suppliers of postal services by using the Internet and getting information from the Post Office. Produce a simple leaflet comparing costs and delivery times.

Organising and supporting meetings

There are several administrative tasks needed to support meetings. You will need to book and set up a meeting room, prepare and distribute the paperwork needed such as **agenda** and **minutes**, and clear the room after the meeting. Any refreshments should be organised beforehand. If there is to be food, check how many people are attending, the time food is required, and whether anybody has special dietary requirements.

Interpersonal skills Needed to communicate with and relate to other people effectively.

Skills and abilities

You will have to use a range of practical and **interpersonal skills** to complete administrative tasks. You will need good communication skills such as listening and questioning, the ability to present a positive image, and skills in time management, problem solving and using technology.

Activity 4

Every job requires specific skills. What particular skills are required to performs each of these job roles:

- customer services assistant in a department store
- accounts assistant for an estate agent
- receptionist at a dental surgery?

It is important to find out what a job is really like. Ask your supervisor if you can talk to other employees in the organisation and ask what they do and don't like about their jobs.

Functional Skills: Using ICT

You will use ICT skills in Activity 3 when researching suppliers of postal services using the Internet.

Just Checking

* Name four administrative processes.
* List the skills needed for two different administrative job roles.

Topic 2.3 What are business communications?

Let's Get Going

Think about the last two times you communicated with a business. This could be a communication on the phone, in person or in writing. Why did you need to communicate?

Communication is the process of sending and receiving messages between one person or group of persons and another. It is important for businesses to communicate with their employees, customers, suppliers and shareholders as well as the tax authorities and other stakeholders. In this section you will learn about the main communication methods used in business.

At work, common reasons to communicate with people are to:

- request information, e.g. the date of a meeting
- provide information, e.g. prices for products
- give instructions, e.g. how to use the new photocopier
- take instructions, e.g. to order new office supplies
- attract potential customers, e.g. by advertising in a newspaper.

Most communications are two-way process. The receiver provides some response or feedback to the sender of the original message. Of course, in a conversation, this pattern is repeated many times.

Formal communication channels are based on an organisation's needs and business requirements. The channels are normally regulated and/or planned by the organisation. An example is confirming a customer order by letter.

Channels of communication

There are three main channels: written, spoken and electronic. Table 2.2 sets out the main advantages and disadvantages of each channel. Note that electronic communications such as emails and mobiles phones are also forms of written and spoken communication. However, they have been separated in the table because electronic communication has specific advantages and disadvantages.

Channel	Advantages	Disadvantages
Written: Letters, memos, reports, agendas, notices, invoices, orders	Permanent record Used for both simple and complex messages	Often takes some time for message to arrive Slow or no feedback
Spoken: Face-to-face meetings, seminars, briefings, appraisals, grapevine	Provides instant feedback Opportunity for discussions	No permanent record Can be time wasting and costly
Electronic: Emails, video conferencing, mobile phones	Rapid transmission Accurate	Can be expensive if technology fails

Table 2.2: Channels of communication

Some business communications are **formal**, while others more **informal**. The level of formality is partly determined by the subject of the communication. You would also use more formal language when speaking to your manager or a customer than when chatting with a friend.

Informal communication channels are based on the needs of individuals and groups. These can satisfy social needs, and usually develop spontaneously. An example is a casual conversation with a colleague.

Why communications fail

Communications can fail for many reasons. Effective business communication depends on each step in the communication process being successful and the correct channel being used.

The sender

The sender can often be the cause of failure. The message may simply be poorly expressed or lack clarity. The message may be too complicated, or it may be so badly presented that it does not hold the receiver's attention.

The receiver

The receiver may be unreceptive to the message. Someone may be too busy or distracted to listen properly or to read the message carefully.

The channel

The channel may be the cause of communication failure. For example, a telephone call may not be understood because the line is poor or cut off in mid discussion. Some computer communications can fail because a file gets corrupted.

PLTS: Creative thinker

Choosing suitable communication methods in Activity 4 will require you to be a creative thinker.

Activity 5

Choose suitable channels of communication to transmit these messages:

- details about a social function at work
- an invitation to a job interview
- a change to the procedure for processing expense claims
- a request for suggestions about how to improve record keeping.

Just Checking

* Name three communication channels used by businesses.
* Sketch the communication process.
* Give two reasons why business communications can fail.

Topic 2.4 Business letters

Letters are one of the main ways a business communicates with others. Letters are useful for formal communications with business contacts, explaining complex matters, and are useful for the recipient as they will have a record of the communication. When someone is talking to you, then you can ask that person to explain what they mean if you don't understand something. You don't have the same opportunity to check what the message means with written communications so they must be easily understandable. Therefore many business letters use standard layouts for clarity.

Let's Get Going

Study some business letters you have received or ask for permission to look at those that have been sent to family members. In groups, discuss what makes a good business letter.

The layout of a business letter is important. It should help to get the message across, but must also look professional, with accurate content, grammar and spelling.

A business would use headed paper for formal letters. The layout is usually determined by a set of standards known as the **house style**. This would usually specify the way documents should be organised, including the typeface to be used. The aim should be to create a positive image of the company.

House style The rules and standards for the design and writing of documents.

Figure 2.3 shows a standard layout for a business letter. The letter may show the organisation's name, address, telephone and fax numbers, website address, logo and any other information such as quality accreditations or awards held by the organisation.

Accepted conventions

There are some accepted conventions that should be followed when producing business letters.

- Don't print complete phrases or sentences in capitals. Text in capitals is much harder to read than standard lower-case text.
- Don't use typefaces smaller than 10 point. Putting extra space between lines will always increase readability.
- Use formal language. You must check the draft letter carefully for accuracy, spelling and grammar, as mistakes will come across as unprofessional.
- Avoid **jargon**, and only use technical language if it is appropriate and you are certain it will be understood by readers.
- If you start the letter with "Dear Sir/Madam" then the close should be "Yours faithfully". If the salutation uses the person's name the close should be "Yours sincerely".

Jargon Terminology, often buzzwords, relating to specific activities or groups. Jargon can be a barrier to effective communication. It can be used to show you are a member of a group or to exclude outsiders.

Wilson Opticians
41 Bond Road
Southampton
SO14 9PH

Mrs J Wilby
8 Norton Green
Southampton
SO14 6DY

4th December

Dear Mrs Wilby

Re: Contact lenses check-up reminder

I am writing to advise that your contact lens six monthly check is now overdue. It is important that you have regular check-ups to ensure the lenses are correctly fitted and eye health is maintained.

Please telephone us on 01262 376498 to arrange an appointment.

Yours sincerely

Lucy Waters
Branch Manager

Figure 2.3: A standard layout for a business letter

Activity 6

Draft a letter from a sales manager to a customer. The letter should confirm receipt of an order but advise there will be a delay of two weeks for despatch due to supplier problems. The letter will be signed by the sales manager. Use a word processor and a letterhead template (provided by your teacher/tutor) to create the letter. Check for accuracy, spelling and grammar, then split into pairs and check each other's letter.

@work

Examine the headed paper of your work placement organisation. Find out whether there is a house style for layout, fonts and sizes.

Just Checking

* Name five uses for business letters.
* What is jargon?
* Why shouldn't you use jargon in business letters?

PLTS: Creative thinker

By adapting styles of written communication you will be demonstrating skills as creative thinker.

Functional Skills: Reading

You will use your reading skills to compare, select, read and understand texts.

Functional Skills: Writing

Activity 6 will require that you use writing skills.

Functional Skills: Using ICT

You will use your ICT skills when using software applications and entering and formatting information. Remember to apply editing techniques when producing information that is fit for purpose and audience, using accepted layouts and conventions as appropriate.

Topic 2.5 Other written business communications

Let's Get Going

Think about other written forms of communication. In groups, discuss the audiences best suited to receive each type of written business communication.

Letters are just one of the methods that a business can use in its communications. The other methods of written communication also have their own conventions in terms of layout. They are useful in many contexts, both for a business's internal communications (with its employees) and its external communications (with its customers, suppliers and others).

Emails

An email is a message sent electronically to another person. Emails can be written very quickly. They are a very immediate form of written communications, and tend to be informal and written in note form. However, there are accepted rules or "email etiquette" which apply when sending business emails.

- Do not attach unnecessary files.
- Do consider whether email is the best way to send a 30-page document.
- Do not write in CAPITALS.
- Do not overuse the "Reply to all" option.
- Do not use emoticons ☺ in business emails.
- Do check spelling and grammar.
- Do not copy a message or attachment without permission.

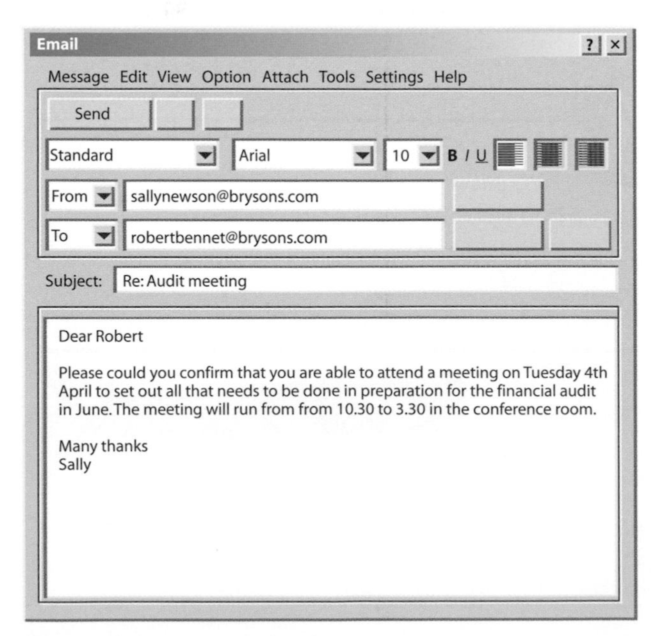

Figure 2.4: A typical email

Memos

Memos can be used for making arrangements and for requesting or sending information. However, as emails also suit these purposes, memos are not used as often today. As a paper-based rather than electronic form of communication, memos are still useful in organisations in which employees do not have regular access to a computer. They are an easy communication tool, although there is no proof of receipt and they do not permit immediate feedback.

There is a standard layout for memos (see Figure 2.5), As with letters, memos must be accurate, grammatically correct and free of any spelling mistakes. You can use informal language but try to be specific and concise in your subject line. In most cases a memo needs no salutation (such as "Dear Sir") or closure.

MEMO

TO: All Staff
FROM: Marjorie Spencer
DATE: Monday 14 June
SUBJECT: Health and safety training

Due to the building extension work taking place, all staff will be required to attend a health and safety training session. This will take place next Monday lunchtime (12.30-13.30) in the new premises. A buffet lunch will be provided.

Figure 2.5: A business memo

Activity 7

Word process a memo to your teacher or tutor listing the do's and don'ts of sending emails. You should use a standard memo template or create one of your own.

Messages and notes

When taking messages from a telephone call or a visitor, it is important that your notes are accurate. Write down the main points – you don't have to use full sentences. Remember to check you have taken all the necessary details, and that the message is written correctly and legibly. Some organisations provide pre-printed forms (see Figure 2.6) that staff should use when taking messages.

PLTS: Creative thinker

By adapting styles of written communication you will be demonstrating skills as a creative thinker.

Functional Skills: Writing

Activity 7 will require you to use your writing skills.

Functional Skills: Using ICT

You will use your ICT skills when sending emails, producing memos using software applications, and entering and formatting information. Remember to apply editing techniques when producing information so that it is fit for purpose and audience. Always use accepted layouts and conventions as appropriate.

MESSAGES

Date: 10 May Time: 10.30 am

Rosie: Matt from Finance called

Monthly car mileages need to be in by 3pm today
Phone him on xtn 415

Kim

Figure 2.6: A form for taking messages

Faxes

Fax machines are used to send an exact copy of a document instantly to another location, which can be anywhere in the world. Faxes are useful for sending copies of letters, diagrams, and drawings.

Forms

Forms are not just used for taking messages. Most businesses use many other types of form to make administration easier. By using a printed form for invoices, purchases orders and other procedures that support trading, a business can ensure that its financial records look professional and capture all the required information.

- Purchase order – this is issued by a business when it wishes to order goods or services from a supplier.
- Invoice – this is issued by a business to a customer making a purchase. It provides a proof of purchase, setting out details of what has been purchased and the price.
- Delivery note – this is delivered with any goods that are dispatched to a customer. The form has a space for the customer's signature to show that goods have been received. The signed copy should be returned to the business.
- Credit note – this is sent to a customer when a business returns money (or credits a customer's account) because it has overcharged the customer or supplied faulty goods (which have been returned).
- Statements of account – this is an up-to-date statement of a regular customer's transactions and sets out the amount that the customer owes the business.

Jellypops

Invoice

Unit 2a
West Aimley Ind est
Didlet
Lower Hatchet
Cambs

Ship to: Dibley
Company Hs
Didlet
Lower Hatchet
Cambs

Invoice Date: 21/08/09

Invoice Number: 125200

Salesperson	P.O. Number	Ship Date	F.O.U Point	Ship Date

Quantity	Description	Unit price	Amount
		Subtotal	
		Total rate	
		Post/Pack	
		VAT	
		Total	

Make all checks payable to Jellypops

Thank you for your business

Figure 2.7: A sales invoice

Activity 8

What do you think are the advantages and disadvantages of using different written methods? Make a list then discuss with a partner.

Functional Skills: Speaking and Listening

Activity 8 will require you to use speaking and listening skills when discussing the advantages of different written communication methods.

Your work experience placement is a useful source of information. Talk to colleagues in different departments and ask them to show you the business documents they use in their jobs to communicate with other staff, suppliers and customers.

Just Checking

* List the different forms a business can use to administer its trading activities.
* Describe four business email etiquette rules.

Topic 2.6 Managing information

Let's Get Going

Why is it important to record information correctly? What would happen if the scanner at a supermarket checkout did not record all the goods being purchased by customers? Discuss the consequences to the supermarket of this type of error.

Businesses hold information about their customers, suppliers and finances. Administrative staff need to manage the information contained in documents sent and received by the business. They must record, store and manipulate information efficiently.

Managing information on a computer

Most businesses use computers rather than paper-based systems to manage information. In this topic you will examine how to record and store information and save text files on the computer.

Organising computer files

When producing business documents using a word processing system, you will need to save them in folders for easy retrieval. In topic 2.2 you looked at ways of organising manual filing systems. Some of same considerations apply to electronic files.

Many organisations have set procedures for naming and organising computer records. You should follow these rules. However, if you are allowed to choose file names, use a system that allows you to find and retrieve files easily. For example:

- use logical file names
- make the file name as descriptive as possible
- include the date in the file name.

If you are unsure where a document has been filed, you can use a file-handling program to illustrate the directory structure of the computer and to find files.

On a PC with Windows, you can use Windows Explorer to find files. Click on "Start" and then "Programs", and your directories and folders will be displayed in the left-hand pane of a split screen. Clicking on a folder will give you a list of files in the right-hand pane. On an Apple computer, you can use the "Find" option to look for the locations of files with particular names.

Saving text files

It is very important to save documents. If there is a power loss or a problem with the computer, you could lose all unsaved work.

Ideally you should set up your programs to automatically save documents at regular intervals, perhaps every five minutes. You should also manually save before undertaking any task that might "go wrong", such as inserting an object from a different folder or using a new untried formatting option.

When saving, you should also make back-up copies by saving your files to a **memory stick** or other storage device. However, note that in business many companies do not allow staff to use personal memory sticks for data security reasons.

Memory stick A removable storage device that plugs directly into a computer through a USB port.

File extensions

You may want to share documents with somebody who does not use the same software as you. These files can be saved in rich text format (with the file extension *.rtf*), which saves all common formatting commands, and in a text-only option (with the file extension *.txt*), which saves the text without formatting.

Editing text files

You should check all written business documents carefully. Poor quality documents could damage a business's image.

Spelling can be checked using a spellchecker facility. However, this cannot be relied on to pick up all errors. For example, the spellchecker will not pick up instances where you use "there" rather than "their".

You need to be familiar with the formatting features and functions of your word processing program. Most programs like Word have a formatting toolbar with buttons for select common commands such as bold, italic or underline. When editing text you may need to combine information from different documents. You can use the help option if you do not know how this can be done.

Activity 9

Using a word processing program, write a memo to your teacher or tutor describing how to edit and save text files. Save the document in different format types using sensible file names.

Functional Skills: Using ICT

You will your ICT skills when word processing and editing text using software applications.

Functional Skills: Writing

Activity 9 will use your writing skills when constructing the memo to your teacher.

Just Checking

* List three points to consider when choosing file names.
* How can you check where your document is filed on the computer?

Topic 2.7 Planning work

Let's Get Going

In groups discuss what methods you could use to help you plan work.

When providing administrative support you will work with other people. Your team may have been given several tasks to complete. Some may need to be done immediately, some may not be so urgent. You will need to plan your work, by setting priorities, agreeing deadlines and deciding who does what. In this section you will look at some of the ways that work can be planned.

All businesses need to plan all aspects of their operations. Administration is no different from any other business function, and good planning is essential for the smooth running of the office operations.

Setting priorities

A good starting point is to first decide what needs to be done, and then decide the order in which tasks need to be done. For example, when working in an office, list things that you need to achieve in the next month. Then you can make a plan for the week ahead. At this stage, you can make a day-by-day plan that should only include those things that you are going to each day. To help you prioritise further, you split each daily plan into three sections:

- "must do"
- "should do"
- "could do".

	Must Do	Should Do	Could Do
Monday	Weekly sales report	Update quality manual	Filing
Tuesday			
Wednesday			
Thursday			
Friday	Check staff rota		

Figure 2.8: Planning activities for the week

It is important that you write the plan for the following day before you finish work each afternoon. If you leave this until the next morning, then you might get too busy and lose control of the day.

Meeting deadlines

On many occasions you will be set deadlines for work. For example, a manager might ask you to complete a task by the end of the day, or to produce a report by the middle of week. You will need to estimate how long each job will take so that you can plan your work to meet deadlines. If a report takes three days to prepare, it is no good starting it on a Tuesday if it is needed by Wednesday lunchtime. It is important to be realistic about what you can achieve, so that you allow a reasonable time in which to do your work.

You should appreciate that failing to meet deadlines can affect other people's work. However, if you meet your deadlines, you will not only be appreciated by your manager but by your colleagues. This builds good working relationships, which will be helpful in a crisis. For example, sometimes you may have to negotiate a revised deadline to deal with an emergency or some unexpected work. You may need to arrange cover for someone who is suddenly taken ill.

Setting objectives

Most businesses set objectives for what they want to achieve. Sometimes these objectives are quite vague, such as "to make a profit". However, it is good practice in business to be more precise about what you want to achieve. One way of doing this Is to set "SMART" objectives. A SMART objective is:

- specific – it clearly sets out what is to be achieved
- measurable – success can be measured, usually in numerical terms
- achievable – the objective is realistic
- relevant – the objective relates to the business's overall goals
- timely – the objective should be achieved within a given time frame.

For example, "to make a profit of £10,000 in the next six months" is a SMART objective. It sets out a much more precise and measurable objective for a business than simply "to make a profit". If you are setting objectives for your own work, you should consider making these SMART objectives.

The production meeting

Kimberley has been asked to help the production manager plan a meeting for 10 regional managers. These managers will have to travel from all over the UK to the meeting. The meeting will be held in three weeks time (on day 21).

Kimberley decides which activities need to be completed to set up the meeting. She draws up a list of tasks and a schedule (setting out when each task should be carried out). Table 2.3 shows this schedule. (Note, the production manager first approaches Kimberley about the meeting on day 1.)

Task	To do
Book venue and organise refreshments (needs confirming five days prior to the event)	Days 1–5
Invite people and send agenda	Day 5
Arrange accommodation for those needing it	Day 5
Organise documentation for printing – need 6 days	Day 15
Confirm those attending	Day 20

Table 2.3: Preparations for the production meeting

How has scheduling her work helped Kimberley?

What changes could you suggest to improve this schedule?

Planning aids

You can use several aids to help you organise administrative work. For example, many offices use a wall planner to help then organise staff work rotas or holiday leave. These planners are especially useful for tasks that need to be planned around regular events in the business year, such as an annual general meeting, year-end and quarterly financial reports, and monthly team briefings.

Electronic organisers are also widely used. These can be as memory joggers, giving reminders of appointments, and as an aid to prioritise and plan work, blocking out time for completing important tasks. They can sometimes be used to access work colleagues' diaries electronically, making it easier to arrange meetings and co-ordinate work schedules.

Figure 2.9: A wall planner

PLTS: Self manager

In the case study, when carrying out planning activities and organising your time and resources, you are demonstrating skills as a self manager.

What planning aids are used in the office in which you are undertaking your work placement? Make notes of the different aids, describing their purpose and recording your views on how useful they are.

Functional Skills: Writing

Recording your opinions in @work will require that you use your writing skills.

Just Checking

* What is a SMART objective?
* Name two different types of planning aids.

Topic 2.8 Using office equipment safely

When working in an office you are likely to use a range of equipment including computers, printers, photocopiers and telephones. You need to know how to use this equipment properly and safely so that you do not harm yourself or damage the equipment.

Let's Get Going

Every workplace has health and safety risks. In groups, discuss what types of health and safety issues could arise in an office. What measures could be put in place to reduce these risks?

Computers

When working on a computer, good posture is very important. Figure 2.12 shows the best posture to adopt.

Figure 2.10: The correct posture to adopt when using a computer

It is important that you take regular breaks, preferably every hour, when using a computer. Spending too long looking at the screen can strain your eyes and cause discomfort.

PLTS: Independent enquirer

When investigating how to use equipment safely and sitting correctly at a computer you will be demonstrating skills as an independent enquirer.

Activity 10

Sit at a computer and practise adjusting the seat and monitor to achieve the correct posture.

Printers

To use a printer safely, you must know how to deal with common problems such as paper jams, a printer being out of paper or toner, or offline. Get someone to show you how to use the printer, and familiarise yourself with the instruction manual. Remember not to misuse a printer by, for example, printing off personal information that could contravene the Data Protection Act.

Photocopiers

When you use a photocopier, make sure you are shown how to use features such as double-sided copying, collation of pages and stapling. If you are lifting boxes of printer paper, make sure you know how to lift them safely (see below).

Telephones

Telephones may not seem like a health hazard, but it can be easy to trip over badly positioned telephone wires in an office. Make sure that there are no wire trip hazards around workstations. You will need to learn the essential telephone functions, such as how to forward calls and set up messages. Use instruction manuals or get someone to show you how the office telephone system works.

Safe lifting

Bad backs afflict many people. Anyone who lifts or moves equipment or supplies incorrectly can suffer injuries and get back pain. In an office you could hurt yourself when moving a box of paper, so it you must know how to lift objects correctly.

The Health and Safety Executive publishes a useful guide on its website (www.hse.gov.uk). This describes safe practices and what employers need to do to comply with the Lifting Operations and Lifting Equipment Regulations 1998.

Talk to the person responsible for health and safety in the company. Ask what procedures are in place for the safe operation of office equipment. Examine your work area and describe the health and safety risks. Write simple instructions for a new team member on how to use office equipment safely.

Just Checking

* Why is it important to use office equipment safely?
* What is the correct posture when using a computer?

Hotlink

The Health and Safety Executive website has information on using office equipment safely as well as general information on workplace health and safety issues. Visit it at: www.hse.gov.uk

Did you know?

Each year in the UK, 80 million working days are lost because people are off work with bad backs. This figure could be substantially reduced if all employees learned safe lifting techniques.

Functional Skills: Using English

You will use your speaking and listening skills in order to check how to use office equipment safely.

Functional Skills: Using ICT

You will use ICT systems to follow and understand the need for safety and security practices.

Topic 2.9 What is a team?

Teams bring together people with different skills that are needed for a project or an area of work. Teams share a common goal and every team member should be committed to working together. In this topic, you will consider what makes a team.

A team can be defined as a group of people with complementary skills, working together to achieve a common goal. In a business context, it has been shown that people who work in a team can be more efficient and effective. They produce better work, both in terms of quality and quantity. This has obvious business benefits.

Let's Get Going

Working in small groups, discuss what you think makes a good team in an office environment.

Figure 2.11: Pressurised environments make effective teamwork even more important

Teamwork

Teams are used in business to bring together people with different skills and abilities to meet specific objectives. For example, a team of people might be brought together to run a clothes and shoes store and help to drive up sales. People in the team will have different roles. The idea is that the sales assistants can work more effectively if the shelves are kept replenished by a stacker. The stacker keeps an eye on stock levels, and when goods are running out, tells the order clerk know to arrange for new supplies.

Teamwork involves working in collaboration with others towards common goals. Teams can be temporary or permanent. A retail business may set up a temporary team to organise a store refurbishment. A care business might set up a permanent departmental team to provide care services for elderly people.

Teams can be any size – the key is to get the right number of people to allow the team to function effectively and to meet its goals. An international company that sells computer and office equipment to other businesss might set up a UK-based sales team comprising four regional managers, each with their own teams providing administrative support such as processing orders, answering the telephone, and filing.

Sometimes teams can become too big and too difficult to manage. Sometimes even the addition of one more person can cause difficulties: a one-person business may function very well but then might struggle if another person comes in to jointly manage the business. The trick is to find the right balance of numbers and abilities that suit the task the team has been set up to perform.

Team development

In business, as in some sports, teams need time to gel together. They go through several distinct development stages. Management experts have called these:

- forming
- storming
- norming
- performing.

At the first stage, the forming stage, members are finding out about each other, and seeing how they fit into the group. They are finding out about the task and objectives, perhaps relying on the leader for guidance, and establishing the group culture.

The second storming stage is where conflict may develop as team members try to jostle for position. If this is not resolved, the group may drift along without a clear sense of purpose. In the norming stage, people start to work together. Previous conflicts are resolved, and the team members develop mutual trust – they speak and listen to each other.

The fourth and final stage is when teams really perform at their best. People will feel they belong, solutions are found, ideas are implemented, and most importantly, proper teamwork is achieved as team members work towards a common goal.

Activity 11

Think about a team in which you have been involved (either currently or in the past). Has this team changed in any way? Did team members always work well together? Were there any tensions or problems between members? Try to describe how this team developed.

Hotlink

This website has lots of ideas for team building activities: www.businessballs.com

Just Checking

* What is the difference between a group and a team?
* List four stages of team development.

Topic 2.10 What makes an effective team?

Let's Get Going

Have you ever been in a team that was not performing well? This could be at school or college, such as a sports team, or hobbies such as a drama group. In groups, discuss your experiences of working in teams. What do you think are the benefits of working as part of an effective team?

When managers set up a team in a business, they will select people with the skills and qualities needed to fulfil the team's goals. They will also try to ensure that they select people who can work well together. Of course, this does not always work out in practice. In this section you will explore what makes an effective team and what happens if there is disharmony in the team.

It is not easy to put a good team together. The combination of personalities, and individual strengths and weaknesses, may cause conflict or disharmony. In some sports, for example, you don't always get the best team by simply picking the best players. You need a group whose members can work with each other.

This means that putting a team together can involve compromise. It is helpful to understand team roles, and how these can be managed to enable teams to develop and maximise their efforts.

Team roles

Team members need to be selected both for their technical and specialist skills, and their preferred personal working styles.

It is perhaps easier to understand the requirement for technical and specialist skills. Each member of a team is qualified to fulfil specific functional roles.

Each member will also have a preferred style of working or performing in a team situation. Table 2.4 sets out nine typical roles that people adopt when working in teams. An individual will feel more comfortable in some roles than others. Each role contributes in its own way to the success of a team.

Successful teams will have a mix of these team roles. A team full of co-ordinators would not be successful because everybody would be fighting to act as leader. However, a team without a good leader or co-ordinator may also struggle to succeed.

These team roles simply provide a guide to how people behave in teams. It doesn't mean that there must be at least nine people in every team – one in every role. Most people can adopt or take on several team roles at the same time. Some teams also call for a greater emphasis on some roles than others. If, for example, you are part of a team of four organising a school outing to a theme park, you would need to agree the venue, make the

Team role	Characteristics
Shaper	Gets things done
Co-ordinator	A good chairperson; recognises strengths and weaknesses of the members
Plant	Full of new ideas
Resource investigator	Good communicator
Team worker	Cares for individuals and the team; good listener; resolves social problems
Implementer	Good organiser
Monitor evaluator	An accurate judge of the situation
Completer finisher	Makes sure everything is done
Specialist	Provides expert knowledge and skills

Table 2.4: Team roles

travel arrangements, book the tickets, collect the money and let everyone know details of the trip. Which roles do you think would be needed to make the trip a success?

Think about the roles that you tend to adopt in team situations. This will give you an idea of the personal strengths that you can bring to a team. Can you see the roles that some of your colleagues prefer when working in teams? What are their strengths?

The best teams don't just make use of each member's technical skills (what they can do) but makes good use of people's strengths (their preferred roles and ways of working).

Effective teams

An effective team recognises the importance of each member's contribution. Team members should also be committed to the same aim or goal. Members of an effective team display:

- trust
- loyalty
- honesty
- supportiveness
- commitment.

Effective teams make a difference to an organisation's performance. Through making the best use of people's differing skills and strengths, teams can improve productivity. They also reduce risk, as teams are better placed to cover the work of someone who is absent. This is why a business like a supermarket chain might put together a team to look after the training and

Motivation The driving force that makes you act the way you do. The energy you put into an activity is related to what you expect to get out of it.

development of its employees. It is likely to be a fairly large team with one section responsible for performance monitoring, another for recruitment and selection.

Teamworking is also a good way to generate new ideas, leading to creativity and innovation. In business, teams have been good at finding ways to improve systems and procedures. Employers find that staff working in teams have stronger **motivation** and greater job satisfaction. A good team spirit has benefits both for a business and for its staff.

Communicating in team situations

Team members need to communicate well if the team is to achieve its goals. Communication involves behaviour and interpersonal skills as well as spoken or written language. In teams, you may have to adapt your behaviour in some situations. Suppose, for example, that a team member is always late getting in to the office or is perceived to lack commitment. This might cause friction in the team. The others would expect the team member to change.

Activity 12

Think of different situations that could cause conflict in a team. Discuss these with a colleague, and suggest ways that each situation could be resolved.

Not all conflict is destructive. Sometimes team members can argue a point very strongly before agreeing on a course of action. This is fine providing the discussion is about the issue, and arguments do not become personal.

In these situations, you need to be careful not just about what you say but the way you say it. Body movement, gestures, facial expressions, posture and eye contact are all indicators of how a person is feeling and thinking. Next time you are sitting in a café look at the body language of other people and see if you can guess what they are feeling. Are they happy or sad or angry?

It is important that you support other team members by showing respect. You should be polite and co-operative. For example, do not interrupt when other team members are speaking. Demonstrate with both words and body language that you are paying attention (unless, of course, you want to convey a different message!). To "tune" into another person, you should face them squarely, adopt an open position, lean forwards, maintain appropriate eye contact (in some cultures this is not acceptable) and relax. Try this with a partner in class. Notice the body language; what does this tell you about how your classmate is feeling?

Figure 2.12: You don't need to speak to convey your feelings

Responding to feedback

Feedback from other people lets you know how well you are doing or how you could improve your performance. It is very useful for team members to be able give and respond to feedback in an appropriate way.

When somebody is commenting on your work, listen carefully. Try to avoid acting defensively or jumping in to justify what you've done. Receiving positive feedback for a job well done is to be enjoyed. But if the feedback is negative, then you should ask for specific examples of performance that could be improved and how you could do better in the future.

Activity 13

What motivates you? What motivated you to do this course? Do you know what motivates individual members in your group? Does being a member of a team motivate you? Make notes and share your findings with other members of your group.

PLTS: Team worker

By communicating with others during Activity 12 you will be demonstrating skills as a team worker.

Ask a few colleagues whether they enjoy working in teams. Ask what they like about it, what they don't. Get their views on what makes a team effective, and how it helps their job and the organisation. See if you can identify the different "team roles" that people have.

Functional Skills: Using English

You will use your speaking and listening skills when taking part in team activities in Activity 13 and @work.

Just Checking

* Name six typical "team roles".
* Identify team role(s) that you are comfortable in.
* What strengths do you bring to a team?
* List three advantages of working in an effective team.

Kaileigh Slater started her own jewellery making business over two years ago. She specialises in designing exquisite necklaces. Her business has several regular customers, including large department stores and exclusive fashion boutiques.

Ali Thomas set up his jewellery business to produce gemstone rings for a mail order company. Recently Kaileigh and Ali decided to form a partnership to combine their skills and expand the business.

Kaileigh and Ali have named the new venture Kali Jewellery. They have a new phone number and website www.kalijewellery.co.uk.

A part-time administrator, Sharon, is hired to help out. Sharon sends a letter (Figure 2.13) to a customer. When the customer receives this letter, she is angry and cancels her business.

Kaileigh and Ali then decide to recruit a full-time administrator. They have drafted a list of activities that need to be carried out:

- answering the telephone/taking messages
- sending out information such as price lists
- keeping the website updated
- handling the mail
- sending out invoices
- ordering stationery.

The administrator should also know the correct way to produce business documents and to check for accurate grammar and spelling.

Tasks

1 Create a standard business letter that Ali and Kaileigh could send to their existing customers to advise them of the new contact details and benefits of the new jewellery partnership. Use standard document conventions in your letter. Check for accuracy, grammar and spelling. Save the letter using a sensible file name and print out a copy of the letter.

KALI JEWELLERY
4 Hampton House
Hampton Business Park
Tollerdown
DT8 5LB

Tel: 01309 483561 Email: kali@jewellery.co.uk

Our Ref: 124/KS

Jennifer Smithers
12 THe Swannery
Hop Streeet
Tollerdown

Dear Jen

I have been asked by K Slater to write to you asking for payment of your overdue invoice. This amounts to £652.26 and I have to advise that if you have not jpaid the bill within the next seven days, then we shall be forced to take action against you.

Please respond to this letter.

Yours faithfully.

Sharon Wells
Administrator

Figure 2.13: The letter sent out to the late-paying customer

2 Figure 2.16 shows the letter sent to a customer who is always late paying her invoices. Give reasons why the customer would be angry on receiving it. Draft a letter that will achieve its purpose without making this customer cancel her business with Kali Jewellery.

3 Prepare a job advertisement for the full-time administrator position to go in the local newspaper.

4 Prepare a checklist for interviewing prospective administrators. Make a list of the different types of business communications. What is their purpose? What should be included about standard document conventions?

PLTS: Creative thinker

By adapting styles of written communication – letters, job advertisement and checklist – you will be demonstrating skills as a creative thinker.

Functional Skills: Reading

You will use your reading skills to compare and understand texts.

Functional Skills: Writing

This case study will need your writing skills to produce different types of document.

Functional Skills: Using ICT

You will use your ICT skills when using software applications and entering and formatting information.

I want to be ...

... a receptionist

Name: Billy Jenkins

Age: 19

* Where do you work?

I work in a dental practice in the town centre.

* What do you do in reception?

I deal with enquiries from people who either phone or come into the surgery. I also arrange appointments, answer calls and take messages, welcome patients, keep patient records updated and secure, order supplies and process payments for treatments.

* Do you work in a team, and if so who else works with you?

There are four dentists, two hygienists, three dental nurses and myself. Three of the dentists only work three days a week, as they are consultant orthodontists at the hospital two days a week. It is a really friendly atmosphere and we all get on really well.

* What do you most enjoy about your job?

I really enjoy working in a close-knit team and being able to meet different people every day. I like the variety of tasks the job offers, especially as the practice is expanding next month to include a chiropractor clinic and I will hopefully be having a part-time assistant to help out. That will help me develop supervisory skills.

* What is the hardest part of your job?

Seeing emergency patients waiting for a dentist when they are in obvious pain and distress. We do pride ourselves that emergencies will be dealt with urgently, and I sometimes have to explain to other patient that their appointments may be slightly delayed. Most people are sympathetic.

* What qualifications and skills do you need?

To work in reception you need to have at least GCSE A*-C in English and maths. Admin and IT skills are also useful. When I was at college I achieved a Business, Administration and Finance Diploma at Level 1. I had work experience in a clothing store during college, which helped greatly in developing my customer service skills. Since working here I have gained an NVQ Level 2 in Customer Services.

Assessment Tips

This unit is assessed by an assignment, which is marked by your teacher or tutor. The assignment has to be carried out at the end of the unit to ensure that you have gained the necessary skills and knowledge.

This unit will be assessed by a single assignment connected to working in a team to plan and produce some written business communication for a business.

You will be required to work as a team, showing your teamworking and communication skills in order to:

- plan your work as a group and an individual
- produce different types of written business communication while using office equipment safely.

You will then review the team activity. This will involve responding to feedback from your teacher/tutor, assessing how well you and your team worked together while carrying out administrative activities and identifying other processes that need to be carried out to ensure the smooth running of an organisation.

For the first part of the assignment, you will be working in groups. You will need to demonstrate your ability to work and communicate in a team, showing fairness and consideration to others. It is important that you keep diary notes of your activities so that they can be referred to later. You should also record your feelings. Write up these notes while the experience is fresh in your mind. Your teacher/tutor will watch what you do and write a witness statement on your performance.

You need to work on your own to produce business documents, using word-processing skills. Your teacher/tutor will watch what you do and write a witness statement confirming how well you use office equipment. For example, you may write a business letter on a computer, save the document in a sensibly named file, print out a copy, then photocopy it to send to different people. To do this you will have used a computer, printer and photocopier.

For the review activity you will need to work on your own. You will have a one-to-one review with your teacher/tutor, where you may refer to the notes you made about the team-working activity. Think how well you worked together as a team – what went well, what could have been better. You can also think about the different organisations you have visited or researched as part of this unit, and can look back at any class notes made about the different administrative activities that help to ensure the smooth running of a business. Your tutor will write a witness statement recording how well you can assess the team activity, how you respond to feedback and how well you know different administrative activities.

What you have learned in this unit...

Learning outcome	Summary	You should be able to
LO.1 Know administrative processes used in businesses	In this unit you have learned about the day-to-day administrative activities that need to be undertaken in an organisation such as: • dealing with visitors • handling mail • organising and supporting meetings • managing manual and electronic information • dealing with enquiries • using telephone systems.	✔ identify administrative processes
LO.2 Be able to produce simple business documents	You have learned about the ways to communicate with colleagues and customers, and the purposes, types and ways to produce different business communications.	✔ manage information ✔ select appropriate formats for business communication ✔ communicate in writing using appropriate language
LO.3 Be able to plan and carry out administrative work safely	You have learned about ways of planning to help manage your time to meet deadlines. You have learned the correct and safe way to use: • computers • printers • photocopiers • telephones.	✔ organise time and resources ✔ use office equipment safely
LO.4 Be able to work as part of a team	You have learned the features of an effective team and explored what makes an effective team member.	✔ work as part of a team showing fairness and consideration ✔ communicate in a team situation ✔ deal positively with feedback ✔ assess team effectiveness

Personal Finance and Financial Services

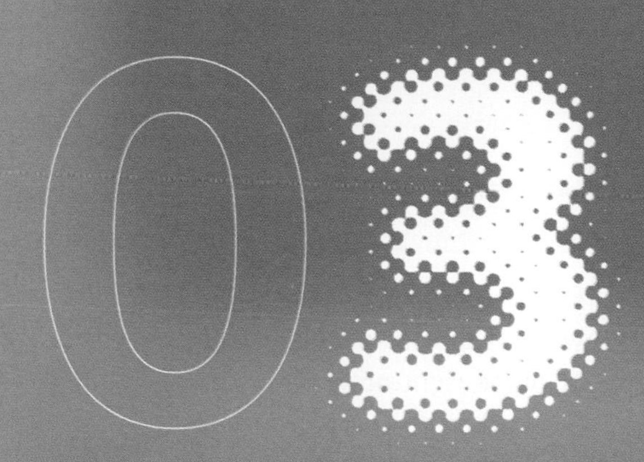

Understanding how you manage your own personal finances will provide a good knowledge base for business. This unit will investigate a range of money-related issues and cover different aspects of finance and financial services. You will look at some of the services provided by financial institutions. You will consider why it is important to avoid getting into debt. You will learn where you can get help and advice about financial issues.

What you will learn in this unit

Assessment

This unit is the externally assessed unit. This means that it will be assessed through an examination with a range of question types.

Topic 3.1 What is money?

It seems good to start a unit on finance by asking a basic question: what is money? Money is a system of exchange. We exchange money for things we want or need. For example, a customer might give (pay) a hairdresser £25 in exchange for the hairdresser using her skills to cut the customer's hair.

Let's Get Going

How much money have you got in your pocket or purse right now? How often do you pay for things each day? What things do you buy regularly?

The currency of the United Kingdom

The currency of the UK is made up of coins and banknotes. There are four main banknotes in circulation – the £50, £20, £10 and £5 notes – and eight different coins – the £2, £1, 50p, 20p, 10p, 5p, 2p and 1p coins.

Modern UK currency is easy to work with because it is calculated using the denary system (multiples of ten).

- £1 = 100 pence
- £10 = 1000 pence
- £100 = 10000 pence

Functional Skills: Maths

Completing this activity without a calculator will demonstrate that you can use a range of mental methods.

Activity 1

You have been given some bank notes and coins. The exact number of each denomination is given in the table below. You need to fill three envelopes with different amounts. These amounts are also given in the table. You must use the right combination of currency to put the exact amount of money into each envelope.

Complete the grid indicating the currency you will put into each envelope. You should have nothing left over when you finish.

Notes and coins	£20	£10	£5	£1	50p	20p	10p	5p	2p	1p
Number available	14	3	2	8	1	5	1	1	3	2
Envelopes										
• £156.33										
• £73.41										
• £99.99										

Legal tender

The term legal tender is used to describe any coin or banknote that can officially be used as money in the UK. Other countries' currencies are not legal tender in the UK. For example, US currency (dollars) is not legal tender in the UK.

The government takes steps to prevent the production and circulation of counterfeit (fake) money. All banknotes have special features that make them difficult (but not impossible) to copy or reproduce. You will consider some of these physical features of cash in topic 3.2.

Did you know?

Coins and banknotes are produced by the Royal Mint. As well as making all the usual coins and notes, the Mint produces some special editions for occasions such as royal weddings and the Olympics.

Types of money

You do not always have to use cash – physical notes and coins – to buy goods and services. As well as cash, there are other types of money. Table 3.1 sets out the different types of money that are commonly used.

Type	Description
Cash	Banknotes and coins. Cash is usually used to pay for relatively inexpensive items. A customer is very unlikely to use cash to buy a new car.
Cheque	Cheques are pre-printed forms that can be used to pay for goods and services. The account holder simply adds the name of the person being paid, the date and the amount.
Debit card	A debit card is used to make electronic payments for goods and services using a plastic card and a PIN (personal identification number). It is a good alternative to cash.
Credit card	A credit card looks like a debit card, but instead of taking the money from a bank account, the cardholder borrows money from a business. It is like a loan.
Credit	Credit agreements are often used to buy expensive items, such as cars or furniture. This is not the same as a credit card, because this credit cannot be used in other stores.

Table 3.1: Types of money

Credit cards and credit agreements have to be carefully managed. Although they can be used to "buy" goods and services, the customer incurs a debt that must be paid back over time. You will owe money to the credit card company when buying goods on a credit card. You will owe money to the store (or sometimes a finance company) when buying goods on a credit agreement. Account holders must make sure that they can manage these debts. They will usually be required to make regular repayments to clear the debt over a period of time. You'll find out more about debt in topic 3.5.

Activity 2

With two or three of your classmates, create an A4 poster that explains the five different types of money to a group of Year 8 learners. Use images to enhance the poster where possible.

Functional Skills: Develop, present and communicate information

This activity will show that you can bring together information to suit content and purpose and present information in ways that are fit for purpose and audience.

Other things that work like money

In addition to cash, cheques, debit and credit cards, there are other forms of "money" that allow you to purchase goods and services.

Loyalty cards

Some shops and stores give loyalty cards to customers. These are designed to benefit customers who use the stores regularly. Each time a customer makes a purchase and presents their store card, the system records the items bought and adds points to the customer's account. Usually the more you spend, the more points you receive. These points can be exchanged for vouchers or gifts.

Loyalty cards

Tesco, Boots and Sainsbury's have led the way with loyalty card schemes. Table 3.2 lists the cards that are issued by each of these stores.

Card	Website
Nectar	www.nectar.com/NectarHome.nectar
Tesco Clubcard	www.tesco.com/clubcard/clubcard/
Boots Advantage	www.boots.com (and click on Advantage Card link)

Table 3.2: Three well-known loyalty cards

Check out each of the websites listed in Table 3.2 to answer these questions below:

- How many points do you get for each pound you spend?
- What benefits do you get from having the loyalty card?
- What can you do with the points you earn?

Vouchers

Vouchers can be useful presents for friends or relatives when you don't really know what else to get them. Each voucher has a specified monetary value. Some specify the type of product that must be purchased. For example, book tokens can be used in participating stores to buy books. Some vouchers can only be used to buy goods from the business that issued the voucher.

Travellers' cheques

When you travel abroad, it can be more convenient to take travellers' cheques than foreign currency. Travellers' cheques can be exchanged for cash at a bank (you pay a handling charge) or for goods and services such as hotel and restaurant bills. These cheques offer more security than carrying large amounts of cash. They can be replaced if they are stolen and unused travellers' cheques can be cashed in when you get home.

Electronic money

Electronic money (or e-money) is a system that allows people to store money on electronic equipment that can be scanned by a reader when you buy goods and services.

Season tickets

Season tickets are a way of paying in advance for transport (and other) services. By paying in advance, you often get a discount. For example, it can be cheaper to buy a season ticket than paying individual fares on buses and trains when you actually travel.

Savings stamps

Savings stamps are available to help people spread the cost of larger bills like the television licence. People like stamps because once they have bought them they cannot use the money for something else!

Just Checking

* What coins are used in the UK?
* What is the definition of legal tender?
* List three of the five types of money.

Topic 3.2 Notes and coins

We are all familiar with coins and banknotes. We use money to buy products and services in shops and from businesses. But what are the features of cash? Why is cash designed the way it is?

Let's Get Going

If you have any cash in your pocket, take it out and look at it now. How do the coins compare? Are they the same size, colour and weight? Do they have the same features? What about the notes? Do they have the same images? Can you see the watermark on a banknote?

Security features

Each denomination (or type) of UK coin and banknote is designed to look different so that we can easily tell them apart. However, they also have some common features. Some of these features are security features to prevent forgery.

Watermark

All UK banknotes bear a watermark of the Queen. A watermark is an impression made on paper during the printing process.

Metallic strip

All UK banknotes also contain a metallic strip. This strip is almost woven through the paper layers and is clearly visible.

Signature

When paper money was first used, each note was signed by hand by the issuing authority to indicate it was genuine and legal. Today banknotes still contain a signature, although this is printed not signed by hand. Banknotes issued by the Bank of England are signed by the bank's chief cashier.

Newly printed £20 notes bear some additional features designed to prevent forgery, including:

- a holographic film strip bearing the number 20
- marks that can be detected using an ultraviolet light
- raised print areas.

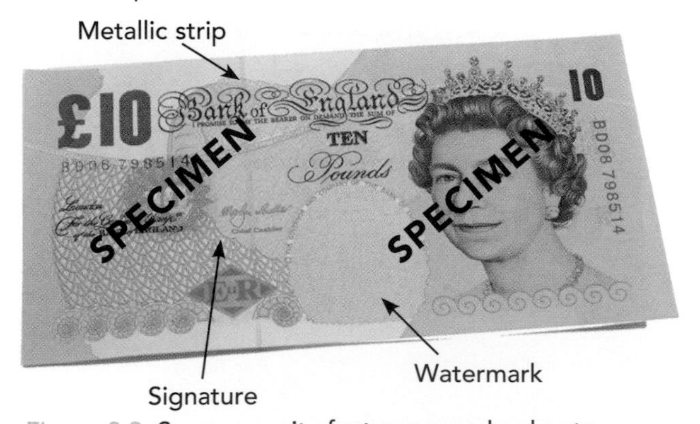

Figure 3.2: Some security features on a banknote

Other features

Although it is important that criminals should not be able to copy money easily, there are other design considerations when producing notes and coins. Most importantly, money should be easy to use.

Coins are designed so that we can tell them apart easily. The weight and size of each type of coin is different. For example, £1 coins are thicker than the smaller value coins. This makes it easier, even for people with poor sight, to find the right change.

Many machines use the fact that each coin has a different weight to count money. For example, vending machines weigh the coins that have been inserted to check that a customer has put in the right amount of money.

Portability

Cash would not be very useful if it was difficult to carry around. Notes and coins must be very portable. In other words, they must not be too heavy or too large. You should be able to carry cash easily. Money is designed to be carried around in a purse or wallet or in a pocket

Durability

Money needs to last. It is designed to be used again and again. This is what we mean when we say that notes and coins should be durable.

Banknotes do not last as long as metal coins. A metal coin that has been through a washing machine is likely to come out undamaged. The same cannot be said of a UK banknote. Banknotes are withdrawn from circulation as they become torn or tattered and are replaced by the Bank of England with newly printed notes.

Some countries, including Australia, New Zealand and Romania, produce banknotes from a kind of plastic called polypropylene rather than paper. The plastic notes are much more difficult to tear. They are resistant to dirt and they can even survive being put in the washing machine!

Just Checking

* List the main security features of banknotes.
* What is a watermark?

Hotlink

You can find more information about UK notes on the Bank of England's website. Use this link: www.bankofengland.co.uk/banknotes/index.htm

This section of the Bank of England's website has a downloadable leaflet about the new £20 note. It has information on how to identify counterfeit currency and other educational material, including a short video about checking banknotes called *Take A Closer Look.*

Topic 3.3 Cheques, bank cards and credit

Let's Get Going

Do you have a savings account? Do you have a card that lets you take money out of your account through a cashpoint? Do you have a passbook that you need to show at the counter? Do you receive statements telling you how much you have in your account? How often do you receive statements?

Many times it is more convenient or more secure to pay by cheque or credit and debit card, or to obtain goods under a credit agreement. For example, it is much safer to send a cheque rather than cash through the post.

Cheques

Banks issue books of cheques to account holders. Each cheque contains printed details about the account, including the sort code (the unique identification code for the bank or building society), the account number, the name of the account holder (this could be a person or an organisation such as a business), and the cheque number.

It also includes space for the account holder to write in payment details when the cheque is used. Cheques must be written in ink.

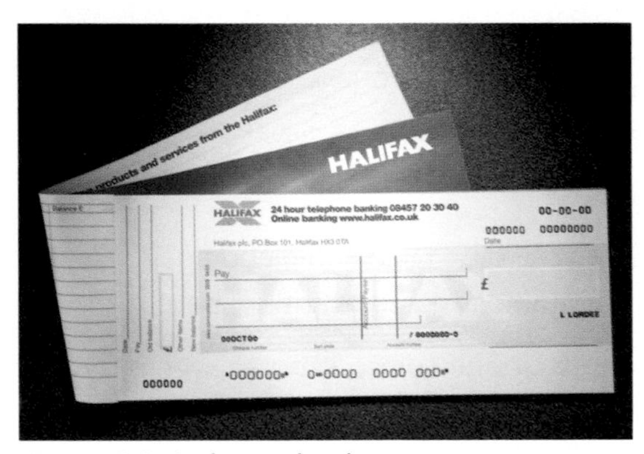

Figure 3.3: A cheque book

When someone wants to make a payment by cheque, the account holder fills in:

- the name of the person or business to be paid
- the amount to be paid in words, such as *Three pounds and twenty-three pence*
- the amount to be paid in numbers, such as *£3.23*
- the date (usually the current date, although cheques can be postdated, that is, with a later date).

The person (or business) being paid must present the cheque to a bank. It can be paid into an account in the name of the person (or business) written on the "pay" line. When the cheque is processed, the money is then transferred into this account from the account of the person who wrote the cheque. It usually takes banks about four or five working days to make the transfer.

Credit cards

A credit card is a flexible loan. When you pay for something using a credit card in a shop, the credit card company actually makes the payment to the shop. In effect, you have been loaned the money by the credit card company. You no longer owe the shop anything, but you must repay the credit card company.

Each credit card customer is given a credit limit. This is the total amount that they can borrow. The customer is issued with a card that enables them to make purchases from any business that accepts credit card payments. The total purchases cannot exceed the credit limit. If the customer has reached the credit limit, the card cannot be used until some of the outstanding debt has been repaid to the credit card company.

Each month, a customer receives a statement showing the balance (the amount owed), the minimum payment that they need to make this month and the date on which this has to be paid. Customers can choose to pay the total balance. If they repay this balance in full, they will not owe the credit card company anything until they use the card again.

Once the monthly payment has been made, the balance is reduced accordingly. The credit card company will charge interest on any outstanding amount. This interest will be added to the next month's statement together with any new purchases that the customer has made with the card.

Debit cards

Although debit card transactions are processed in a similar way to credit cards, there are important differences in the flows of money. When you pay a store using a debit card, money is directly transferred from your bank account to the store's bank account. There is no "third party" involved, such as a credit card company.

Each time you use your debit card you are making a transaction – money is being taken from your account. Each transaction you make is recorded and displayed on your bank statement.

Many businesses prefer customers to pay by debit cards rather than credit cards. This is because credit card companies charge

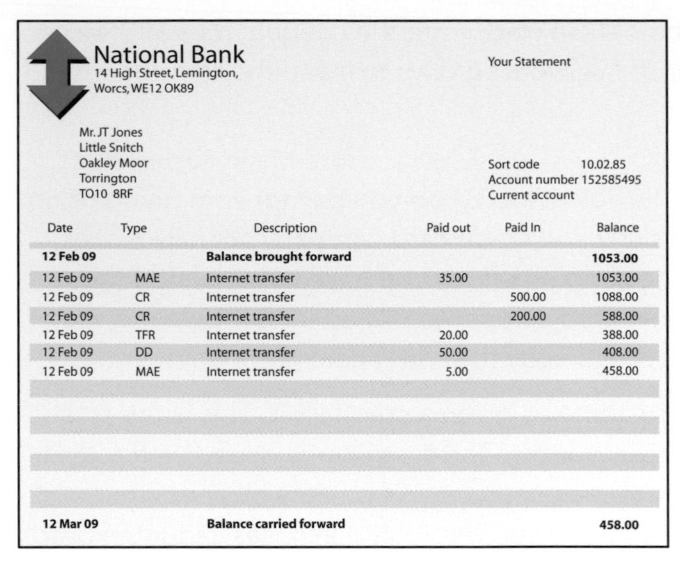

National Bank
14 High Street, Lemington,
Worcs, WE12 OK89

Your Statement

Mr. JT Jones
Little Snitch
Oakley Moor
Torrington
TO10 8RF

Sort code 10.02.85
Account number 152585495
Current account

Date	Type	Description	Paid out	Paid In	Balance
12 Feb 09		**Balance brought forward**			**1053.00**
12 Feb 09	MAE	Internet transfer	35.00		1053.00
12 Feb 09	CR	Internet transfer		500.00	1088.00
12 Feb 09	CR	Internet transfer		200.00	588.00
12 Feb 09	TFR	Internet transfer	20.00		388.00
12 Feb 09	DD	Internet transfer	50.00		408.00
12 Feb 09	MAE	Internet transfer	5.00		458.00
12 Mar 09		**Balance carried forward**			**458.00**

Figure 3.4: A bank statement

businesses a small commission when they process a transaction. When you pay a business by debit card, the business receives the full amount you have paid. This is why some businesses may charge you a little less if you pay by debit card rather than credit card.

Store and other forms of credit

As well as using credit cards, you can also use other forms of credit to make purchases. These other types of credit are usually one-offs, an agreement for an exact amount to buy a specific product. To get credit, a person must have a good credit history. This means that the customer must have a good record of paying back any previous loans that they have taken out.

A mortgage is one type of credit agreement. It is a loan used to buy property, such as a house, flat, factory or office. The amount borrowed is secured against the property. This means that if the person who takes out the mortgage does not make the agreed repayments including interest payments, the bank or building society can repossess (legally take back) the property. Mortgages are only available to buy property. The interest on mortgages is generally quite low in comparison to that charged on money borrowed for other purposes.

Many clothing stores have their own store cards. Customers will sign up for a card to buy items from that shop on credit. Monthly payments need to be made in the same way as credit cards or interest and late payment fees will be added. The interest rates on store cards are usually higher than those for bank loans and credit cards from banks.

Credit agreements are often used for occasional expensive purchases. Car dealers will offer customers credit when buying new cars. The customer borrows money from a credit company to buy the car, and pays it back by making regular payments. Just like with a mortgage, if the customer fails to make the payments, the car can be repossessed and sold.

Some stores draw in customers with 'interest free credit'. These promotions allow customers to pay the set amount as long as it is paid back within a set period. However, the interest charged by many other finance companies for car loans and other credit agreements is usually higher than the interest rates charged on bank loans.

Activity 3

Find advertisements for a bank or building society loan and for a major credit card. These could be adverts in newspapers and magazines or on television. Find out the interest rates being charged by both organisations – the bank/building society and the credit card company.

Write down the repayment period for the loan – the period of time over which you borrow money. Find out (or calculate) how much you will need to repay each month if you borrow £5,000.

Just Checking

* Which takes money directly out of your bank account – a credit card or a debit card?
* Can cheques be written in pencil?
* What happens if you do not make repayments when you buy goods on credit?

Functional Skills: Reading

When you investigate websites and read information it will show that you can understand texts in detail.

Topic 3.4 Where does money come from?

Let's Get Going

Who gave you the money you have in your pocket at this moment? Where did they get the money from? Do you have any savings? If so, where did these come from?

All businesses need money to fund their operations. Entrepreneurs need to find ways to finance their ideas. Here are some suggestions on how money can be raised.

Sources of money

In this topic you will look at some of the ways in which people can get money.

Personal sources

Most people obtain money from personal sources. People earn money through their work, but this can also be supplemented with money from other sources. Table 3.3 sets out some of the ways that money can be generated.

Source	Description
Earned income	Earned income (or pay) is what you receive when you have a paid job.
Inheritance	A sum of money, property or other assets that is left to another person when someone dies. Usually people leave money to members of their family, close friends and partners. If you inherit a large amount of money, you might have to pay some of it in tax.
Selling	Selling personal belongings through car boot sales or auctions is an easy way to raise money. The modern version of the car boot sale is the website eBay (www.ebay.co.uk).
Borrowing	You may be able to borrow money from banks and building societies, credit card companies and other financial institutions. You can also borrow from friends and relatives. However, you should remember that you have to pay back whatever you borrow.
Saving	You put money into a bank account so that it will gather interest and be available when you need it at a later date.

Table 3.3: Financial sources

Banks and other lenders

Before banks and building societies existed most people were paid in cash, which they kept in their homes. However, this wasn't very safe for obvious reasons. Money could be easily lost or stolen. Banks provided a more secure place to keep money.

Some bank customers chose to keep their money in the bank for long periods of time as savings. Banks found that they could lend some of this money to other customers who wanted loans. Savers were paid interest for keeping their money in the bank, and borrowers were charged interest on their loans. Banks are an important source of finance for businesses and individuals.

Building societies were originally created specifically to lend money in the form of mortgages to people who wanted to buy property. Banks now offer mortgages too. How do you make decisions about which bank or building society to choose when you want to open an account? Section 3.8 will give you some suggestions on the criteria you could use to help you decide.

Figure 3.5: Banks are present in most high streets and shopping districts

State benefits

If you are unemployed and you meet certain criteria, you can claim state benefits. How much you get will depend on the reason why you are unable to work and your personal circumstances. The actual amount you will receive will be quite low.

Benefits in the UK are currently paid to the unemployed who are looking for work, the disabled and the long-term sick (ill or injured). You might also qualify for some financial support if you are on a very low income.

Activity 4

With a partner, visit the online auction site www.ebay.co.uk. Find out what sorts of products are bought and sold on eBay. List 25 different types of product or service that are bought and sold on eBay.

Create an A5 user guide that gives basic information to new eBay users about what they can do on the site and provides simple instructions on how to make a bid.

PLTS: Independent enquirer, creative thinker and team worker

Investigating eBay will demonstrate your skills as an independent enquirer. Deciding on the content of the user guide will show that you are a creative thinker. Working with your partner will show that you have skills as a team worker.

Just Checking

* How do banks get money to lend to customers?
* List two reasons why people can claim state benefits.
* What is an inheritance?

Functional Skills: Reading

When you investigate websites and read information for inclusion in a document like the user guide it will show that you can understand texts in detail.

Topic 3.5 What is debt?

Let's Get Going

Do you owe anybody any money? When do you intend to repay it? How will you get the money to repay the loan?

Have you borrowed money telling the other person you will pay them back? Maybe a friend did something for you, and you said: "Thanks, I owe you." In either case, technically you are in debt. A debt is something owed. When you talk about debt you usually mean money, but it can refer to anything that is borrowed.

Managing debts

Debt is not always a bad thing. In fact, most people will incur debts in their life. As we showed in topic 3.3, a debt is incurred every time a credit card is used. People incur a debt when they take out mortgages to buy a home, or borrow money to go on holiday or buy a new car. Businesses often borrow money – and so go into debt – to finance new ideas and expansion plans.

Debts only become a problem if they are not properly managed. It is important therefore to avoid getting into too much debt. Borrowers are usually required to make regular repayments. Failure to do so can result in legal action. Several organisations provide advice on making financial decisions and can help people with debt problems. You will review some of these organisations in topic 3.6.

Hotlink

The Citizens Advice Bureau provides practical advice on debt issues on its website. Visit: www.adviceguide.org.uk/index/life/debt.htm

Avoiding legal action

There are consequences if you are unable (or fail) to pay your debts. Your **creditors** will take action. They can take you to court to try and force you to pay.

If the debt is against a car or a home, the court can order that this property can be taken back (repossessed) by your creditors. For example, if someone fails to pay their mortgage, the mortgage company can repossess their home. The property is then sold. The proceeds from the sale are used to pay the outstanding debt on the mortgage.

Figure 3.6: If people don't manage their money, they can find that debts quickly mount up

The courts can also deal with other types of debt, such as unpaid credit card bills. The court may instruct bailiffs, who are paid to recover property and debts, to enter a home or business to remove items that can be sold to repay debt. Under law, you must let bailiffs into your property. If you refuse, they may return with the police. There are strict guidelines about what bailiffs can remove from a home to repay debts. Essential items cannot be taken but they can take televisions, DVD players, games machines and mobile phones.

Most businesses only take legal action as a last resort. However, it is obviously best if you can avoid getting into debt problems in the first place. If you do have difficulties paying your debts, talk to your creditors. This is much better than doing nothing and hoping the problem will go away.

Creditors are the businesses or individuals that you owe money to if you go into debt.

Avoiding added costs

If you find it difficult to pay your debts, you can face additional costs. If you do not make the required repayments your **creditors** may demand additional money on top of what you already owe. It is likely that if you are taken to court, you will have to pay both the original debt and the court costs. The amount the court instructs you to pay is known as the judgement. It is far better not to get yourself into this position in the first place.

Hotlink

www.moneyfacts.co.uk – Moneyfacts offers 10 top tips for getting out of debt.

Maintaining a good credit rating

It is should be straightforward to maintain a good credit rating. As long as you pay your bills on time and keep up your payments on loans and other credit, there really should be no problem. If you don't, you will get a bad rating. A poor history will make it difficult for you to obtain credit (and/or a mortgage) when you need one.

You can also experience problems if you suffer identity theft. This is where your personal details are fraudulently used by someone else to obtain credit to purchase goods and services. This person can then run up debts in your name. It can be very difficult to clear your personal credit history when this happens.

Activity 5

Together with three or four others, research, plan and film a short three-minute video or podcast on debt and how to avoid getting into debt problems. You will need to write the script, and either act the parts yourselves or persuade others to act them for you.

PLTS: Independent enquirer, creative thinker, team worker and effective participator

Working with a group to research, plan and film a video will demonstrate the skills of an independent enquirer, creative thinker, team worker and effective participator.

Just Checking

* What does repossession mean?
* What is a judgement?
* What are the consequences of having a poor credit history or rating?

Topic 3.6 Taking decisions about money

Financial planning is the process of ensuring you have enough money to meet your commitments. It is a key skill in business, but is also important in your personal life. In this topic you will learn that decisions you make about money depend on your age and situation. Topic 3.7 will show you how to budget.

Let's Get Going

What sorts of things do you spend money on? How do you make decisions about what you can afford?

PLTS: Reflective learner

Looking at the financial issues that affect you as an individual will provide evidence of your skills as a reflective learner.

Activity 6

We will face various financial pressures in our lives. The financial commitments we take on – and the way that we pay for them – will depend on our age and circumstances.

- **Early life (under 16):** Almost everything is paid for by parents or carers.
- **Late teens (17–21):** You may enter relationships and have an independent social life. You may go to college or university, perhaps living away from home for the first time. This may be financed by loans or parents and carers.
- **Adult life (22–65):** You may have longer-term relationships, get married or have children. You will probably pay a mortgage (or rent) on a home, and buy cars and household goods.
- **Older age (after 65):** You can retire, but may rely on the state pension and savings. Ideally all debts will be paid off.

Using the information above as a starting point, create an A2 poster of the timeline of a typical life. Use annotated images to show the various factors that influence financial planning at different stages of our lives. Think about what income there will be, and the bills and debts that may need to be paid at each stage. Present the poster to the rest of your class.

Advice and guidance

Many organisations (and businesses) can provide advice and guidance on financial issues.

Banks and building societies

Banks and building societies tend to sell only their own financial products, such as mortgages, loans and insurance. This means that under Financial Services Authority (FSA) regulations, they cannot offer independent financial advice. However, banks can offer general guidance on financial planning.

Independent financial advisers

Independent financial advisers are able to offer guidance on any mortgage, loan and insurance products. They often do not charge directly for this advice, as they receive a commission if you take out a policy with a financial institution.

Citizens Advice Bureau (free financial information and advice)

The Citizens Advice Bureau is a charity. It provides free, impartial (independent and unbiased) advice on issues such as managing debt, state benefits and legal problems. You can access these services in one of three ways:

- online (at www.citizensadvice.org.uk)
- by telephone
- in person through the drop-in and appointment service.

Activity 7

The consumer magazine *Which?* reviews financial products and advises on money issues. Using your school, college or local library, find other magazines that can help you understand money-related issues. Make a list of these magazines and keep a copy in your portfolio.

Just Checking

* What are your financial commitments likely to be between the ages of 22 and 65?
* What advice can you get from a Citizens Advice Bureau?
* What do independent financial advisors do?

Hotlink

www.dwp.gov.uk – Department for Work and Pensions. Gives guidance on benefits and entitlements

www.nationaldebtline.co.uk – The National Debtline. Provides free and confidential advice about dealing with debt problems.

www.moneyfacts.co.uk – Moneyfacts. Allows comparison of different mortgages, credit cards, bank accounts and other financial products.

Functional Skills: Reading

When you investigate the resources available in your library for inclusion in a list it will show that you can understand texts in detail.

Topic 3.7 Budgeting

Managing a budget is an important skill. It provides a good way to avoid getting into debt. This topic will help you to understand what a budget is and how to operate one.

Let's Get Going

Do you budget? When you are given money do you plan how you are going to spend it? Do you stick to the plan? Do you write down what you have spent and what you have left over?

Personal budgets

A budget is a way of monitoring income and expenditure. This technique is used in business but is as useful for planning personal finances. A budget enables you to check that you can pay for things when you need to.

To draw up a personal budget, you need to:

- identify what comes in (from paid work or other sources)
- identify what goes out as planned or unplanned expenditure.

Income	£179.50	wages received weekly every Friday
Rent and bills	£80.00	paid weekly every Monday
Bus pass	£10.50	paid weekly every Wednesday
Food	£40.00	paid weekly (different times)
Total in	£179.50	
Total out	£140.50	
	£39.00	Disposable income

Figure 3.7: **A personal budget**

Figure 3.7 shows a typical budget. The disposable income could be spent or could be saved for unexpected expenses, a holiday, a car or even a deposit for a new home.

Recording your income and expenditure

Keeping records and monitoring your income and outgoings using a diary or spreadsheet will help you to maintain control of your finances. Figure 3.8 shows the monthly finances of the person who prepared the budget in Figure 3.7.

Activity 8

Look at the spreadsheet in Figure 3.8. Regular income and expenses are highlighted. Are there any times when more money is spent than available? What would you suggest can be done about them? How does expenditure compare with this person's budget in Figure 3.7?

Date		Money In	Money Out	Balance
01/09/09	Opening balance			£26.87
05/09/09	Wages	£179.50		£206.37
07/09/09	Rent & bills		£80.00	£126.37
08/09/09	Food		£45.00	£81.37
08/09/09	Shirt and shoes		£65.00	£16.37
10/09/09	Bus pass		£10.50	£5.87
11/09/09	Wages	£179.50		£185.37
14/09/09	Rent & bills		£80.00	£105.37
17/09/09	Bus pass		£10.50	£94.87
18/09/09	Wages	£179.50		£274.37
19/09/09	Food		£56.00	£218.37
20/09/09	Jack & Megan - birthday presents		£40.00	£178.37
21/09/09	Rent & bills		£80.00	£98.37
23/09/09	Mary's wedding		£60.00	£38.37
24/09/09	Food		£35.00	£3.37
24/09/09	Bus pass		£10.50	-£7.13
25/09/09	Wages	£179.50		£172.37
26/09/09	Jeans		£35.00	£137.37
27/09/09	Night out with friends		£30.00	£107.37
28/09/09	Rent & bills		£80.00	£27.37
28/09/09	Cinema tickets		£10.80	£16.57
29/09/09	Food		£15.00	£1.57
01/10/09	Bus pass		£10.50	-£8.93
02/10/09	Wages	£179.50		£170.57

Figure 3.8: Record of income and expenditure

Budget surplus you have more money than anticipated because your expenses are lower than planned.

Budget shortfall you have spent more money than planned so don't have any left.

Budget surpluses and budget shortfalls

A budget shortfall could happen because you had an unexpected expense, or you just spent more than planned on items like food. The best way of handling shortfalls in a budget is to juggle other expenditure or go without something, like eating out, for a while. Of course, you could borrow money from a friend or relative. However, you should be careful when you borrow money, as you will have to pay it back.

A budget surplus is less stressful. This is an opportunity to save some money for unexpected expenses.

Activity 9

Create your own spreadsheet of your income and expenditure. See if you can plan out the next six months. Remember to update the spreadsheet each time you have additional income or expenditure.

Just Checking

* What are the two main parts of a personal budget?
* What should you do with a surplus of money?

PLTS: Self manager

Putting together a finance spreadsheet will show that you have skills as a self manager.

Functional Skills: Maths

Through budgeting you will be able to show that you understand positive and negative numbers in a practical context and that you can solve problems requiring calculation with simple formulae. It will also show that you can work with common measures including money.

Topic 3.8 Storing, saving and investing money

When you are earning money, you will need to decide how to keep your money safe. You may want to save some money. You may want to open a bank account to keep and manage your money, and to use to pay your bills. The choices you make will determine how easily you can access the money and how much you might earn from your savings. In this topic, you will explore some of the options.

Let's Get Going

Suppose you have been left £1000 in a will. You decide to save this money. How would you choose to save it? In groups, discuss the options. What is the most attractive option?

Options for storing money

When it comes to looking after your money, particularly your savings, you have several choices. Table 3.4 sets out the main ways you can save or invest your the money. It describes the main advantage and disadvantage of each method. If you are in any doubt about the best way to store your money, you should always take advice before making any decisions.

Method	Advantages	Disadvantages
At home (probably in cash)	Your money is available when you need it	It is easily lost or stolen
In a bank or building society	The money should be secure	Money in some types of account cannot be accessed outside normal bank working hours
Investing in property	The value of property tends to go up, making it a good investment	Value of property can also go down
Investing in valuables, such as jewellery and antiques	The value of such treasure is likely to go up	Can be difficult to turn into cash
Investing in financial products, such as stocks and shares	You can earn a lot of money in a short space of time	You can lose a lot of money in a short space of time

Table 3.4: Methods of saving money

Banks and building societies

Most people will have an account with a bank or building society. Many employers pay your salary directly into your account. In topic 3.9, you will look at how to open a bank account. In this topic, you will review some of the factors to consider when choosing a bank or building society.

Choosing a bank is not always straightforward, so you need some criteria you can consider when making your choice. However, before looking at these criteria, remember that your choice does not lock you in forever. At various times in your life, you may have different banking needs. You might move between banks, or have more than one account with one or more banks or building societies.

Services

Banks and building societies provide a range of services. Table 3.5 sets out some common services. Some may be important to you, others will have less importance. Are the services that are important to you offered by the institutions that you are considering?

Service	Description
ATM (cashpoints)	These machines allow you to withdraw cash. They also allow you to view your balance and order bank statements.
Telephone banking	Telephone banking allows account holders to access account information and carry out transactions by talking to a bank employee on the phone.
Internet banking	Most banks also now offer Internet banking services. This service enables you to conduct online transactions such as paying bills or checking your balance.
Student friendly	Some banks offer special deals to attract students or provide special facilities for students, such as low interest loans.
Overdraft facilities	An overdraft is a type of short-term credit. It allows you to spend more than you have in your account (so that your balance goes into the red).

Table 3.5: **Bank services**

Internet and telephone banking

Two of the services listed in Table 3.5 are Internet and telephone banking. Some customers find these a more convenient way to access and manage their bank account. If you intend to make full use of telephone or online banking, then you may not need to visit a branch very often. If this is the case, then it will not matter so much whether the bank has an extensive branch network. Indeed some banks such as Smile can only be accessed online. They do not have any branches.

To use these "remote" services, you will need to remember numbers, key presses and passwords that you will have to input when prompted using the keypad on a telephone or a keyboard. If you are using Internet banking, the secure website symbol should be visible on your browser. This is a tiny padlock, which usually appears on the status bar (often on the right of the frame, either at the top or the bottom). If the padlock is shown as closed, it means the website is secure. If it is open, the site is insecure and should not be used to send any financial details. These could be intercepted and used to hack into your account.

Location

If you need to visit of a bank on a regular basis, then you want a branch to be easily accessible. So you may want to consider whether a bank has an extensive branch network. Is there a branch near your home, or near where you work or where you study? Many banks have a branch locator on their website, which you can use to find your nearest branch.

Functional Skills: Using ICT

Using the Internet to gather information in order to support the decision-making process is evidence of your ability to select and use software applications to meet needs and solve given problems.

Activity 10

To use branch locators most effectively, you will need to know your postcode. Visit the websites of these three high street banks and find out which of the three has the most branches close to you:

- HSBC
- Lloyds TSB
- Barclays.

Convenience

Most banks tend to have similar opening hours. Banks are generally open from Monday to Friday and some, but not all, also open on Saturday mornings. If this is the most convenient time for you to visit your bank, then you might wish to limit your choices to those that have a branch open near you on a Saturday.

Supporting products

You should always make sure you know exactly which supporting products your bank will provide. Table 3.6 lists the key products.

Product	Description
Cash card	A cash card can be used in ATM (automated teller machine) to draw cash directly from your bank account.
Debit card	An alternative to cash, debit cards can be used when you buy goods or services from a shop or a business. They can be used either in person or over the phone. Money is taken directly from your bank account.
Cheque	Cheque books are still available from banks if you request them, although most people prefer debit cards because they are secure and more convenient to use.
Paying in books	A paying in book looks like a cheque book, but is used to pay money into an account.
Regular statement	A bank statement gives a breakdown of the activity on the account. It list money paid in and money paid out, and gives the account balance.

Table 3.6: **Products that help you use your bank account**

Interest rates and bank charges

Another important consideration is how much a bank will pay you in interest when you have savings, and how much it will charge you when you borrow money. Banks often offer good savings and/or loan rates to attract new customers. You should check how long these offers last, as many only apply for a limited period.

When you borrow money, the bank may set a fixed or variable interest rate. A fixed rate of interest means that the amount of money you pay each month will never change over the whole time you are repaying the loan. A variable rate means that the amount you pay each month may change over the time you are repaying the loan or mortgage.

Interest rates for overdrafts can be very high. This is why it is good practice to pay off any overdraft at the first opportunity. The bank can also charge you penalties if your account goes overdrawn and you have no overdraft facility.

Figure 3.9: **Debit cards rather than cheques are now used to pay for many products**

Activity 11

Access information on the Barclays Bank Student Bank Account. This can be found by visiting the Barclays Bank website (www.barclays.co.uk) and clicking on "current accounts". Create a short A5 leaflet, designed to appeal to students that explains the features of the Barclays Student Bank Account. Share this with your class and teacher/tutor.

PLTS: Independent enquirer and creative thinker

The research about student accounts will provide evidence that you are an independent learner and using this to produce a leaflet will demonstrate skills as a creative thinker.

Just Checking

* What are the main advantages and disadvantages of cash?
* Why might the location of a bank or building society's branches be important to a customer?
* What is a fixed interest rate? What is a variable rate?

Functional Skills: Develop, present and communicate information

Creating a leaflet that uses a range of different presentation formats and applications will show that you have skills in developing, presenting and communicating information.

Topic 3.9 Opening a bank or building society account

Let's Get Going

Banks and building societies have to carry out some checks when someone opens an account. Why do you think this is necessary? What things do you think they check?

Having chosen a bank or building society using criteria such as those discussed in topic 3.8, you now need to consider how to open an account.

Once they are earning, most people have a current account. These accounts are used by people to manage their money in day-to-day life. In most cases, a person's wages will be paid into a current account and they use the money in the account to pay for living expenses. Banks do not charge customers to use most types of current accounts if they keep their accounts in credit.

People use savings accounts when they wish to put some money away for use at a later date. Money held in savings accounts earns interest each month, which is added to the balance.

Opening an account

To open a bank or building society account, you will need to meet any eligibility criteria, complete an application form and produce documentation to prove your identity.

Eligibility

There are some restrictions on the types of account that individuals can open. There can be age restrictions on some accounts. A young person is unlikely to be able to get a credit card until they are 18. Some accounts must be operated by a parent or carer until the account holder reaches a specific age.

Some accounts are specifically designed for people in employment. These require account holders to make regular payments (such as a monthly salary) into their accounts.

If you are in any doubt that you will be able to open an account, take a parent or carer with you to the bank or building society.

Application forms

When you open the account you will need to complete the account application form, providing some personal information. This might be a paper version but many banks and building societies will allow you to open an account online. However, to complete the process, you will need to visit a branch with your proof of identity.

Proof of identity

To ensure that accounts cannot be opened for criminal purposes such as fraud or money laundering, all customers wishing to open an account have to prove their identity. To do this, you will need to present personal documents such as a birth certificate, a passport or a driving licence. A personal letter or other document with your name on it will not be suitable.

If you do not have any of these documents, you can take someone with you who has been a customer of the bank or building society for a reasonable period (usually at least three years). This person can then vouch for your identity.

Signature

Once your account has been opened, the bank or building society needs to able to check who you are relatively easily. The institution needs to ensure that the person making (or authorising) any transactions really is the account holder. This is why you will provide the bank or building society with a specimen copy of your signature. They can use this copy to check against your signature on cheques and other documents.

You can only sign paper documents. You cannot provide a signature when you use a credit or debit card in a machine or when you make any transactions online or by telephone. You will be given a PIN (personal identification number) for any cards you hold. You will be asked to provide a password or a "memorable word" for electronic and telephone transactions.

Account identification

Just as banks or building societies need a procedure to ensure that you are who you claim to be, they also need a system to distinguish between each account. There are three pieces of information that uniquely identify each account: the account name, the account number, and the sort code.

The account name will be the name of the account holder – if you open an account, it will be your name. The account number will be a unique number allocated by the bank or building society to your account. The sort code identifies the institution and the branch at which you hold your account.

The sort code is made up of six digits, in three pairs, for example 23-12-08. The first two numbers identify the bank or building society; the last four numbers indicate the branch. Table 3.7 shows the two digit identifiers belonging to each of the main high street banks. (The codes of some minor banks are not listed in the table.) So the example of 23-12-08 would be a Barclays account.

First two digits in sort code	Bank
20 to 29	Barclays
30 to 39	Lloyds TSB
40 to 49	HSBC
50 to 59	NatWest

Table 3.7: **Bank sort codes**

When you open your account you will be notified of the sort code (which you will share with the rest of the branch's customers) and your account number (which will be unique to you). These numbers will be printed on each cheque in your cheque book.

You can see a video on how to open a basic bank account on the MoneySense pages on NatWest's website. The MoneySense section of the bank's website is: http://www.natwestf2f.com/natwest/default.asp

Then follow these links:

- click on MoneySense for Schools
- click on 14–16
- click on Bank On It
- click on It's your turn to get banking
- click on Joe opens a bank account

Functional Skills: Writing

Creating a poster is a good example of writing documents to communicate information. You will need to write coherently and include an appropriate level of detail. Don't forget that if the poster is displaying steps or a checklist, make sure that the information is in the right sequence.

Activity 12

Create an A4 poster that lists the steps you need to go through to open a bank or building society account.

Calculating interest and borrowing charges

Once you have opened an account, you will want to keep a check on any interest you may earn. If you have taken out a loan, you will want to know the repayments you need to make each month.

To calculate the interest on savings, you need to know:

- how much is being saved (if it is a lump sum), and/or how much is to be saved each month
- the interest rate being applied
- the period over which the money is to be saved (in months).

Activity 13

Use a savings interest calculator to work out how much your savings will be worth in these two scenarios.

(a) Calculate how much £1000 will be worth after 60 months (5 years), at 6% interest. Remember to set the monthly payments to 0.

(b) Suppose you save £50 each month for 36 months (3 years) at 4.5% interest. How much will you have saved including earned interest after 36 months? Remember to set the lump sum amount to 0.

Hotlink

You can find calculators on the Internet to help you calculate the interest on your savings. For example, visit: http://www.moneymatterstome.co.uk/interactive-Tools/GeneralInterestCalculator.htm

Functional Skills: Mathematics

Activities 14 and 15 will both need mathematical skills to be completed.

To calculate the repayments on a loan, you need to know:

- how much is being borrowed
- the period over which the money is to be repaid (in months)
- the interest rate being applied.

Hotlink

You can find calculators on the Internet to help you calculate the monthly repayments on loans. For example, visit: http://www.moneymatterstome.co.uk/interactive-Tools/LoanCalculator.htm

Activity 14

Use a loan calculator to work out the monthly repayments on a £5,000 loan taken out over 48 months (4 years) at 8% interest. How much will be repaid overall (including interest and the actual repayment of the loan)?

Just Checking

* What is a current account?
* List two types of personal identification that can be used to open a bank or building society account.
* What is a PIN?
* What does a sort code identify?

Topic 3.10 Bank transactions

Let's Get Going

What do you think are the main transactions (procedures) that you can do on a bank account? Make a list of the things that people will want to do with a bank account so that they can manage their money.

You have considered how to choose a bank or building society, and how to open an account. In this topic, you will look at how you might use an account.

Paying in and withdrawing money

You do not need to visit the bank to withdraw money. In fact while some transactions are only possible at the bank counter, many can be done online, over the phone or an ATM. Table 3.8 lists the main transactions that can be undertaken in a bank and at an ATM. Notice that many transactions are the same.

Table 3.8: Transactions available at the counter and at an ATM

Location	Transaction
• At a counter	• Pay in • Withdraw (take out) money • Change your PIN number • Transfer money between accounts • Request statements • Obtain balance
• At an ATM using a PIN	• Withdraw (take out) money • Change your PIN number • Transfer money between accounts • Request statements • Display balance • Top up mobiles

Direct debits

Direct debits are often used to pay bills that are due each month or each quarter. You might have a direct debit arrangement to pay your monthly mobile phone bill. Electricity and gas bills are often paid by direct debit, usually four times a year.

To set up a direct debit you should provide the business to be paid with your bank details and give them authority to request payment from your account on agreed dates. From that point on, your bills will be paid automatically until the direct debit ends or is stopped.

Standing orders

A standing order is another way of making regular set payments to another account automatically. This process is controlled by the account holder, not the business receiving the payment. This means you can stop standing orders at any time.

BACS

Many companies use BACS – which stands for Bank Automated Clearing System – to pay the wages of their employees directly into their bank accounts.

Internet, telephone and postal banking

Many people do not find it convenient to visit their bank on a regular basis. Instead, they use Internet, telephone or postal banking.

The main difference between these types of banking is the additional security. For Internet and telephone banking you may need to set up additional passwords so that your identity can be checked. For postal banking your identity will be verified by checking your signature.

You can carry out most of the same transactions as in a bank. The main exceptions are paying in and withdrawing money. You can pay in money using postal banking, but it is not a good idea to send cash through the post as it could get lost.

Find out what methods your company's customers can use to pay their bills.

Just Checking

* What is a standing order?
* What does BACS stand for?
* What is a direct debit?

Topic 3.11 Protecting against fraud and theft

Let's Get Going

Is your bank account secure? How do you look after your account information? How do you look after your card? Does your bank provide any special measures to help you?

Banks are well protected: few get robbed directly. However, many criminals target individual bank customers. You can be vulnerable to fraud and theft (of your bank cards, for example). For this reason, it is essential that you protect yourself.

Security methods

Banks and building societies implement systems to ensure your personal information is secure. They have procedures that are designed to prevent unauthorised people accessing your bank account. In this topic some of these procedures are outlined.

Customer verification

Customer verification is a system where you provide a password – a sequence of letters and numbers – which the bank holds on file. When a system needs to verify who you are, you will be asked for parts of this information. For example, suppose the password on record is WESTERN167.

During a transaction the system might ask you for the second, fourth and ninth characters of your verification code. If you do not key in the correct answer – ET6 in this case – you would be denied access. At no time will you be asked to provide the whole code.

Secure Internet connections

Many websites begin with the letters http. This stands for Hypertext Transfer Protocol. It defines how web pages are formatted, transmitted and displayed.

A more secure form of this protocol is https – Hypertext Transfer Protocol Secure. Data is encrypted before it is transmitted and it is unscrambled when it arrives at the destination computer. This means the data is not much use to anyone if they manage to intercept it during transmission.

Card reader system

Some banks now issue customers with a card reader device that must be used when banking online (via the Internet). Barclays' device is known as a PINsentry. The card reader is used to make sure that the person doing the online banking has the card for the account and they know the corresponding PIN number.

Figure 3.10: The card reader issued by NatWest to internet banking customers

How account holders can improve security

You should not simply rely on the bank to protect you against fraud. Account holders share the responsibility for the security of their bank accounts. They can take some basic steps to protect against fraud and theft.

Keeping PINs secret

You should never share your PIN information with anybody. This compromises the security of your card. Memorise the number. If you do feel you need to keep a written record of your PIN, make sure you keep this secret and safe.

Secure storage and disposal of documents

Most people keep documents that hold personal information such as bank statements or wage slips for a period of time. The information they have could be exploited for fraud. They should be stored securely, where access for others is difficult. Make sure that they are completely destroyed before you throw them away. A document shredder is probably the most efficient way to destroy your bank statements.

Activity 15

Now that you have finished the unit, test your learning by completing the online quiz on the MoneySense section of NatWest's website. Visit: http://www.natwestf2f.com/natwest/default.asp.

Then follow these links:

- click on MoneySense for Schools
- click on 14–16
- click on Bank On It
- click on Quiz.

How did you do out of 10?

Just Checking

* What does a device like a PINsentry do?
* Why should you keep your PIN secret?
* What is the best way to dispose of sensitive and confidential documents?

Case Study

PLTS: Various

Undertaking the case study will contribute to these skills:

- independent enquirers
- creative thinkers
- reflective learners
- team workers
- self-managers
- effective participators.

Functional Skills: Speaking and listening

Working together will show that you can be flexible in discussion, make relevant contributions to discussions and respond appropriately to others. Presenting your work will show that you are able to communicate in a formal setting.

Functional Skills: ICT – find and select information

If you find a range of materials from different sources you will show that you can select and use appropriate sources of ICT based and other forms of information.

Most high street banks offer online services. The banks give customers choices: they can use the branch network and they can use online and telephone services.

Some banks, however, operate online only.

Choose one of these UK Internet banks to investigate:

- Smile
- Egg
- First Direct
- Cahoot.

What services does the bank offer? Which services do you think are most useful to someone of your age? Would you, for example, need a mortgage or insurance against redundancy?

What sorts of advice and guidance does the bank offer? For example, does it offer advice on security or managing debt? Does the bank offer any benefits like student loans or discount cards?

You have been asked to consider the development of a new banking concept. This is an Internet bank specifically aimed at young people who want to open their first bank account. The company developing this idea wants to create an Internet bank that is uncomplicated and friendly. It should be attractive to students and other young people. It will only offer the services to people in the 16–21 age range.

In teams of four, complete the tasks on the following page. Carry out research, analyse the results and come up with a concept for the bank, remembering to focus on the need for the bank to be straightforward, providing only the most useful services. You should also identify incentives that might persuade people to open an account.

To begin with you should read all the tasks and create a formal plan that breaks down the activities in an appropriate way and allocates the tasks to individuals within the group. Ensure that each time you meet as a group, you begin by checking the activities that have been carried out against the plan. Discuss any discrepancies as a group and reflect on how well you have planned this work.

Tasks

1. Prepare a questionnaire to research into the types of financial products and services that would interest individuals in your age group. Ensure that the questionnaire asks about the types of incentives that might make young people more likely to open an account.
2. Carry out the questionnaire by interviewing at least 10 different people in the target age group. Analyse your results.
3. Use the results of your research to develop a series of advertising and marketing materials. Choose four products or services for further research and development. Choose two incentives that respondents have indicated might make them more likely to open an account.
4. Create a series of A4 advertising posters, each featuring one of your chosen products or services. You should create a name and logo for your bank that can be used on the posters.
5. Create four A5 leaflets or flyers, one for each of your chosen products or services. They should explain the features of each product or service in a way that will attract potential customers to open an account with your bank.
6. Create a PowerPoint presentation to present your marketing material to your bank's management.
7. Discuss as a group how you think the project went. What went well? What went badly? What might you change if you were asked to do a similar project again?
8. Discuss your review with your teacher or tutor.
9. Save the project plan, questionnaire, posters, leaflets and PowerPoint presentation and any notes on your project review to a CD or other storage device. Give this to your teacher or tutor.

Functional Skills: Writing

Checking your work for spelling and grammar will demonstrate your developed skill in this area.

Functional Skills: ICT – using ICT

Using different software applications shows that you can select and use appropriate software. The project will also demonstrate that you can use ICT to plan and organise your work. Backing up the work will show that you can manage aspects of information storage.

Functional Skills: ICT – develop, present and communicate information

Depending on how you organise information in documents you will be able to show a range from this skill set.

I want to be ...

... a payroll clerk

Name: Tanisha Bryant

Age: 19

✱ What does a payroll clerk do?

A payroll clerk calculates the wages and salaries for an organisation's staff. (Wages and salaries are both words for pay – wages are paid weekly and salaries are paid monthly.)

A payroll clerk has to work out the gross wage (the number of hours worked multiplied by the employee's hourly rate), then calculate the deductions for tax, national insurance and pension contributions to give the final net wage figure. The clerk makes sure that each employee gets paid the right amount at the right time.

Another part of my job is to tell the company's head of finance how much tax and national insurance needs to be paid to HM Revenue and Customs each month.

✱ What sort of training did you have?

I completed a Business, Administration and Finance course and then did some on the job training with my employer.

✱ Do you use computers as part of your job?

Yes, I use payroll software to help me, although I have to do some of the basic calculations myself (like adding up how many hours were worked each day to give a weekly total). I learned how to use the software when my employer paid for me to go on a college course. I really enjoyed it.

✱ What sort of skills do you need to be a payroll clerk?

You need to be well organised and methodical. You must be able to keep records and make sure all the time that these records are accurate. You also need to have excellent IT skills and to be really good with numbers.

✱ Do you enjoy being a payroll clerk?

It's a very demanding and busy job and it really makes me feel valued because I am trusted to deal with confidential information.

I always knew that I would go into a career where I would work with numbers!

This unit is externally assessed. This means that you will sit an examination. The examination will be in the form of a graded test with a range of question types. It will last 60 minutes. The mark you achieve for this examination will be your mark for the unit.

You should prepare for this examination by reading through your notes and looking through work you have completed. When you sit the examination you should make sure that you read each question very carefully before attempting to answer it. When you have answered a question it is good practice to read it again and check your answer. When you have completed the whole examination, you should check the whole paper again.

What you have learned in this unit...

Learning outcome	You should be able to	Summary
LO.1 Know the main types, features and sources of money	• identify the types, features and sources of money in everyday situations	✔In this unit you have learnt about different types of money including cash and credit cards. You have considered the various sources of money and you have investigated the services provided by banks, building societies and other lenders.
LO.2 Understand the importance of avoiding debt	• explain why it is important to avoid getting into debt problems • suggest ways of managing debts	✔You have learnt about debt and what can happen if debt issues are not resolved.
LO.3 Know how to plan personal finances	• identify sources of financial information and advice that can be used to help you make financial decisions • construct simple budgets for personal use	✔You have learnt about how your financial needs are likely to change at different points in your life, and you know where to get advice and support for money-related issues. You have learnt about budgets and you know the importance of monitoring your income and expenditure.
LO.4 Know how to choose and use current and savings accounts	• outline how to open and manage current and savings accounts • find out a bank's and building society's information requirements, costs, charges and benefits • select an appropriate current account and a savings account based on the accounts' features • outline security measures taken to protect against fraud and theft	✔You have learnt about products and services provided by financial institutions. You know to choose the right bank or building society to meet your needs and how to open a bank or building society account. You can protect yourself against fraud and theft. You understand and can demonstrate good practice in keeping your financial information safe.

Sales and Customer Service in Business

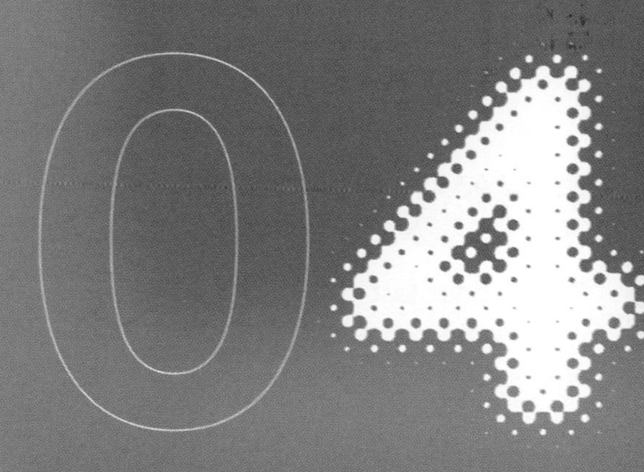

How do you feel when you get good service? What is it like when a salesperson really knows their business and provides a product or service that is just right for you?

If you compare that with how it feels to receive poor service, you begin to understand why a business needs to ensure that its customers are satisfied. Businesses need to make sure that customers get the product or service they want at the right price.

In this unit you will find out about how businesses set out to provide excellent customer service. You will also begin to develop your own skills in customer service and sales so that you can contribute to excellence in customer service wherever you choose to work.

What you will learn in this unit

LO.1 Know the role of sales and customer services in a business

4.1 The role of sales staff

4.2 Sales methods

4.3 Customer service procedures

LO.2 Know how organisations provide effective service to customers

4.4 Understanding customers

4.5 What is effective customer service?

4.6 How is effective customer service provided?

LO.3 Understand the importance for organisations of providing effective service to customers

4.7 The importance of effective customer service

LO.4 Be able to interact with customers

4.8 Dealing with customer enquiries

4.9 Making a sale

4.10 Skills needed when dealing with customers

Assessment

This unit is assessed by an assignment, which will be marked by your teacher or tutor. It will involve you dealing with customers in a sales situation.

Topic 4.1 The role of sales staff

Let's Get Going

Think about last time you bought something. Who sold it to you? Were you impressed by the service? What could the salesperson have improved on? Would you be able to sell that product or service? Discuss your thoughts with a colleague.

Sales staff play a very important role in providing customer service. They are usually the first members of an organisation to be met by potential customers. If sales staff make a poor impression, people may not buy and they may tell others about their experience. This means the business receives bad publicity and fewer customers. Sales staff have to give a good impression and represent the face of customer service for their company.

Selling is a vital activity within a business. If sales are not made, the business will not receive any revenue nor make any profit. A business with poor sales will fail. It seems obvious that a salesperson sells things, but that is not all they have to do. Let's look at all the aspects of their function.

Selling products and services

Did you know?

When you first meet someone, that important first impression is fixed in only 10 seconds. So look smart, stand up straight and smile!

Selling requires several skills. You can learn these skills; they can be taught. Later in this unit, you will find out and practise the skills a salesperson needs.

Remember that salespeople do not just sell physical products but services too. Customers – whether consumers or businesses – need both products and services. For example, a salesperson from a food manufacturer may visit a supermarket to sell it cereals to stock in its stores. Cereal is a product. You can touch it and see it. The same supermarket may be visited by a salesperson from a security company. This company might provide security guards and patrol dogs to protect the supermarket premises at night. This is a service. It is not something that the customer – in this case the supermarket – can take home. Also, it might not be a good idea to touch the guard dogs!

Communicating product information

Figure 4.1: it is important that sales staff create a professional image

Salespeople need to have a very good knowledge of the products and services that they are selling. They must give the right information to customers when they are deciding whether to make a purchase. Sales staff need to know the features of a product – its size, colour, what it is made of, what it does, etc. They also need to know the benefits of any services – that is, how the service can please the customer.

Salespeople must also know the prices of what they sell and whether they can offer customers any possible discounts. They have to know when products can be delivered and what after-sales service is provided.

Table 4.1 sets out the features and benefits of a service. Produce similar tables for two products or services offered by the company in which you have your work placement. Make sure you describe all the features and benefits.

Features	Benefits
Covers UK and Europe	If travelling abroad, you don't have to remember to call the insurance company
Includes roadside assistance	You don't need to take out membership of the AA or RAC
Fully comprehensive	Covers everything – you will be protected even if the accident is your fault
Courtesy vehicle after accident	Gives you convenience at what could be a difficult time
Any driver	You can hand the keys to a friend if you are tired or want a drink

Table 4.1: Features and benefits of a car insurance policy

Supporting customers through the buying process

Customers need to be helped to make the right purchase, particularly if they are spending a lot of money. The salesperson can assist them by answering their questions and by suggesting which product can best meet the individual needs of the customer. Imagine if you had enough money to buy a new car. You might be worried about spending such a large sum of money. The salesperson could help you by giving you all the information you need, by being available on the telephone if you needed to ask questions and by keeping you informed of issues such as delivery. The salesperson can also offer reassurance, perhaps by telling you how you will be assisted if you have any problems after you take delivery of the car.

Organising sales promotions

People in sales sometimes have to organise promotional activities and events. These are often very enjoyable as they get to meet many people and have the opportunity to tell potential new customers about their products. A sales promotion can take many forms, including a free gift with a purchase, a price discount for a limited period or a special event such as an exhibition. The role of the salesperson is to use the promotion as a tool to increase sales. Sometimes, the promotion helps them to "**close**" the sale. This means that by offering the promotion, such as free delivery or a price discount, the salesperson adds that little extra benefit that helps persuade the customer to make a purchase.

Profit The money left over from revenue when all expenses have been paid.

Potential customer Someone who might buy a product or service.

Close Bringing the customer to a buying decision.

Figure 4.2: Expensive products such as boats are often promoted at trade shows

Keeping customer records up to date

A salesperson needs to keep information on products and customers and other records. Can you think what records might be needed? What about:

- details of the customer's name and contact details
- order forms
- invoices
- delivery details.

As well as information about the sales they make, sales staff on the road may have to keep a log of their work, including where they went and how long they spent with **potential customers**. In an office or bank, staff may keep records of how many customers they saw on each day.

Activity 1

Think of someone you know who works in sales. Maybe they work in a bank or in a shop. Perhaps they travel from business to business selling products and services. Carry out an interview with a salesperson using prepared questions. You can make up some of your own questions but these will help you start.

- What products or services do you sell?
- What do you have to know to be able to sell successfully?
- What helps you sell best?
- Do you get involved in sales promotions? If yes, can you give details.
- How do you keep information about customers?

Now make up at least two more questions of your own.

Report back to your group on your interview. If you can, tape the interview as this will help you to remember what your interviewee says later. You can use highlights from the tape to include in your report. Your report can be oral.

PLTS: Independent enquirers

In Activity 1, identifying questions for your interview and carrying out the interview will show that you are an independent enquirer.

Just Checking

* Why are first impressions important in sales?
* What is the difference between revenue and profit?
* Suppose you buy some thick blinds for a living room window. Describe one benefit of this product.
* List two types of records that might be kept by a salesperson.
* What is the difference between an existing customer and a potential customer?

Topic 4.2 Sales methods

In this section you are going to investigate the different sales methods that might be used to sell products and services. Some products are more suited to particular sales methods and some can be sold through various **channels**.

Let's Get Going

Think about all the ways a mobile phone can be sold. You can buy a mobile online from a website that allows e-commerce. You can buy a mobile over the telephone – you might find out information from a website to make your choice and then telephone the sales department of the mobile company. You can go to a shopping centre and visit a one-brand store such as Vodaphone, a phone specialist store such as Carphone Warehouse or an electronic retailer such as Currys. In groups, discuss which approach you prefer. What are the advantages and disadvantages of each method of buying a mobile phone. Write these up on a flip chart.

Personal selling

Personal selling is where the salesperson meets the customer face to face. This can occur in two main situations. First, it occurs where the customer visits the business, such as when you go to the shops. Second, it occurs where the business visits potential customers, such as door-to-door selling.

In-store

Most shops employ sales assistants. Their role is to sell to the customer and therefore they must know about the products on offer. In some stores the salespeople will have specialist knowledge. For example, when buying a personal computer you would expect to get a lot of information and advice. If you were buying groceries you would tend to need less help.

Door-to-door

Today, not many products are sold door-to-door to consumers. However, some businesses attempt to sell products such as double-glazing or building services door-to-door. Most people are very wary of salespeople who call unannounced at their homes. It is always a good idea to check the identity of salespeople before letting them in. Some services, such as insurance, are also sold to consumers in the home, but usually by appointment.

A form of door-to-door selling more commonly used is business to business. Salespeople will visit business customers on their own premises, usually by appointment. For example, Mars, the chocolate and sweet manufacturer, employs salespeople to visit retailers. The sales team take orders and encourage retailers to display Mars products prominently in their stores.

Online sales

Selling goods and services on the Internet is becoming a more and more popular channel for shopping. Products available include holidays, clothes, train tickets and groceries.

Telesales

Telesales is the term for selling products over the telephone. Its success depends to some extent on whether the salesperson is **cold calling** or making calls to a potential customer that has already expressed interest in the product or service.

If, for example, you see an advert for a product that interests you, then you might leave a message asking for further information. When the salesperson calls you back, he or she knows that you have already expressed an interest in the product. This makes the salesperson's job easier. If the salesperson is calling people at random from a list, there is no guarantee that the person being called will have any interest in the product on offer. It is much less likely that the call will result in a sale.

Figure 4.3: A direct mail flyer

Channel The means by which a product or service reaches (or is sold to) the customer.

Response rate The percentage of people who reply to a direct mailshot.

Cold calling Making sales calls (or visits) at random to people who have not previously expressed interest in your product.

Direct mail

Direct mail, also known as junk mail, is when advertising is sent directly to customers in the mail. The **response rate** to direct mail is quite low. Many people just throw it away. It needs to be very interesting and well designed to catch the attention of the person who receives it.

Activity 2

Think of a service that you could offer in your spare time to earn some extra money. It could be a dog walking service, babysitting, baking or cleaning.

Design a direct mailshot in the form of a postcard to distribute to potential customers. Make sure you include your contact details on the card. Discuss your completed postcard with a colleague. Evaluate each other's ideas and recommend improvements to each other's mailshot.

Just Checking

* Give two examples of products where customers would expect to be given plenty of information by the salesperson before committing to a purchase.
* Why is direct mail sometimes called junk mail?
* Why should customers check on the identity of door-to-door salespeople?

Topic 4.3 Customer service procedures

Let's Get Going

A customer service department should be able to answer any question about the organisation's products and services. For example, the Post Office's customer service department might be asked these questions.

- Which is the best postal service for me?
- Where can I get details of current postage costs?
- How long does it take to set up a mail service?
- How do I set up a PO box?

Imagine you wanted to send a Christmas present to a friend in Australia. What questions might you want to ask?

Many companies have a specialist department in charge of customer services. The staff working in these departments are not sales staff. Their function is to serve and support an organisation's customers. To do this, any dedicated customer service department undertakes several common procedures and activities. These are reviewed in this section.

Providing information about products and services

The Post Office's customer service department can provide information about products and services. This is an important activity for any customer services department. Customer services assistants should have access to information about all products and services offered by their company at their fingertips. They will usually be able to access much of this information on their computer. Like salespersons, they must know something about the process – how the product is made, how the service is organised – and about delivery and special promotions too.

Supporting the sales process

Customer service assistants may support sales staff in their work. The salespersons may deal with customers up to the point when they commit to a purchase, and then they will pass customers on to customer services to complete the sales process. Customer services may deal with the payment process and any other matter up to and including the delivery of the product or service.

This is best demonstrated by an example. Suppose Mr Jones goes into a furniture store to buy a leather sofa. With the help of a salesperson, he chooses the model he wants and selects the fabric and the colour. He pays a deposit and fills in papers to pay the rest in instalments on **interest free credit**. He is told his sofa will be ready in 10 weeks and is given a copy of his order. The customer services number is on the form. Mr Jones goes home and realises his stairwell is very small. He calls customer services and asks for the measurements of the sofa. He thinks the sofa will fit up the stairs. Two weeks later Mr Jones realises that he will be on holiday when the sofa is due to be delivered. He calls customer services again. They rearrange the delivery so that Mr Jones will get his new sofa a few days after he returns from holiday.

Interest free credit
A payment plan that allows customers to pay for their goods in regular instalments over a period of time without paying any interest.

Early Learning Centre

Read this extract from the Early Learning Centre (ELC) website and before tackling the questions that follow.

Safe and Sound

All our toys meet or exceed all British and European standards for toy safety.

We test our toys just like your kids do.

We push them down the stairs, throw them, jump on them, knock them over, poke fingers in them and even lick them. So we know our toys are as tough as the children that play with them.

Our Early Learning Centre Stores

Early Learning Centre opened its first store in the mid 1970s and now we have 196 Early Learning Centre stores and 84 shop-in-shops within Mothercare stores across the UK. And when you visit one of our stores, you can take our toys out of the box and play with them, so you can choose the exact toy your child likes to play with best.

Every Tuesday morning, we devote time to our playtime sessions, where your children can join in some real hands-on fun. There are new toys to play with, and lots of competitions and activities. And if you need some help choosing toys, just ask our friendly staff for advice - and look out for great gift ideas and playing tips in store too.

- Which society works with the ELC in developing safe toys?
- How does ELC test its toys?
- What are the Tuesday playtime sessions for?

Go to the Early Learning Centre website (www.elc.co.uk). At the bottom of the home page, there is a set of links under the header "About ELC". Click on the link "About us". Choose three of the services featured on this page. Explain how each of your chosen services is helpful to parents. Present your answers in a word-processed table.

Think of and describe another new service that the Early Learning Centre could offer its customers.

Functional Skills: IT

In completing the tasks in the case study you will need to access the Internet when researching into the Early Learning Centre.

After-sales care

The customer service department takes care of customers after they have bought the product. This might mean giving advice on how to look after the product. It may mean arranging a replacement for damaged goods or correcting an unsatisfactory service. Sometimes the customer service team will need to organise repairs for customers. Good after-sales service can have long-term benefits. It helps to build up relationships with customers. It can produce loyal customers who will want to use the business again.

Did you know?

If a business manages to resolve a complaint efficiently and quickly, it can turn an unwelcome situation into an opportunity. Dealing with complaints promptly and to the customer's satisfaction creates goodwill, and a satisfied customer is very likely to use the business again.

Dealing with enquiries and complaints

Customer services will have to field all enquiries from existing or potential customers. These might come in letters, emails or telephone calls. The customer service team must ensure that all enquiries are dealt with promptly, either by passing the customer to the appropriate department in the company or by finding out and sending relevant information to the customer.

Sometimes customers will have complaints, particularly if products or services have been unsatisfactory. It requires special skills to deal with complaints. Customers may be angry, and customer services assistants must remain calm, tactful and helpful.

Activity 3

Figure 4.4 shows a letter of complaint from a customer. You need to decide what action should be taken and write a suitable reply. Use this template to present your reply.

Light Up
186 Manor Park
Manchester
M45 6GH

Customer's address
Date
Dear ....

Yours sincerely
Jerry Thorpe

Functional Skills: Writing

In Activity 3 you will write a letter in a business format, which communicates information suitable for a customer to receive.

52 Strongbow Road
Denton
Herts
HR3 45Z

Mr Jerry Thorpe
Light Up
186 Manor Park
Manchester
M45 6GH

15 February

Dear Mr Thorpe

I ordered some G10 light bulbs from your online store Light Up. My order ref is 36789. I received some light bulbs from you but they are much bigger than G10 and do not fit my light sockets. I would return the bulbs if you are willing to pay postage and can send me the correct lights.

I look forward to hearing from you.

Yours sincerely

Helen James

Figure 4.4: A customer complaint to Light Up

Just Checking

* Name two sorts of information that a customer service assistant might need to know.
* What is after-sales service?
* What is the business benefit of dealing with complaints well?

Topic 4.4 Understanding customers

Most businesses aim to provide excellent customer service. In order to do this, they must understand their customers.

Customer groups

To understand their customers, a business needs to ask some questions. What type of people (or businesses) buys its products? What are their particular needs? To do this, it is useful to look at specific groups or types of customers and then think about what they might need.

New or repeat customers

The first distinction to make is between existing customers and new customers. Existing customers (or repeat customers) are those who have previously made a purchase from the business. Companies will encourage repeat customers (or repeat business) by ensuring customer satisfaction and providing good service.

It can be more difficult to attract new customers. New customers may need more information to get them interested in the company's products and services. This can be costly, as it may require sales promotions and advertising campaigns.

Individual characteristics

Individual consumer needs vary from person to person. However, it is possible to see some patterns by factors such as age, **gender**, **income** and education.

This is why, for example, businesses target some services for specific age groups. Senior citizens get discounts in some DIY stores on one day a week. Holiday companies provide clubs and activities for children to allow their parents time to relax.

Can you think of any examples of customer service that is linked to gender? What about fashion shops that provide sofas and magazines to occupy men while their wives and partners are shopping and trying on clothes?

Some businesses provide specific services for people on low incomes. Theatres offer **concessions** for people on benefits. Students can get lower fares on trains and discounts in shops. Similarly, businesses may provide a luxury customer service. First class air passengers are offered their own waiting lounge, fast check-ins and high quality food and services on the plane itself.

Let's Get Going

Many companies have "mission statements". These set out what they hope to do in business. Providing excellent customer service is often a theme of a mission statement. For example, Tesco says that "we aim to provide all our customers with excellent value and choice". What do you think is the mission statement of the provider of your course? Can you write one?

Gender Grouping people by sex: that is, male and female.

Income The money received by a person (or household) from their work, benefits, pensions and other sources.

Concessions Price discounts offered to particular groups, such as the elderly, the unemployed or students.

Mobility The ability to get around.

Special needs

Some customers have special needs. A business should ensure that its customer services meet the needs of these customers. For example, retail businesses should be accessible to people with disabilities, such as hearing, visual impairments or problems with **mobility**. These customers may need physical help, such as ramps for wheelchairs, or large print leaflets.

Businesses in the catering, food and restaurant industries may cater for people with special dietary requirements, such as intolerances to wheat, gluten or dairy or even low sugar products for diabetics. Vegetarians are now usually catered for.

Some organisations take steps to cater for speakers of English as a second language. They provide leaflets and information in several languages. Salespeople are trained to be patient, and to listen carefully and speak clearly so that they can be understood.

Think about your work placement or an organisation in which you have worked. What types of customers does it have? Describe any special services provided for each customer type. Record your findings in a table like the one below. This has a couple of typical examples given to get you started.

Type of customer	Service provided
Children	Table and Lego bricks
Visually impaired people	Leaflets in large type

Discuss your findings in groups and think of other services that your chosen businesses could offer its customers.

Did you know?

Tesco finds out about its customers through its Clubcard scheme. Some 14 million people have these cards. Tesco is able to use the information recorded on Clubcards to analyse the shopping patterns and purchases of different types of customers

Just Checking

Using this topic, insert appropriate words into the spaces in the sentences that follow.

A person getting a cheaper ticket gets a ________

To give excellent service a business must understand ________

Shops sometimes offer ________ discounts.

A ________ customer is one who comes back.

PLTS: Creative thinkers

You will generate ideas and discuss possibilities about what services can be offered to different types of customers.

Topic 4.5 What is effective customer service?

It is important that businesses know the difference between poor or excellent customer service. Customers do! In this topic you will study the factors on which customers judge customer service.

Let's Get Going

What do customers want from customer service? A survey asked a sample of customers this question, and these are the top five responses (with the most popular request listed first).

- Customer service staff should have the authority to deal with a problem.
- Customers wanted to talk to a human being (not an automated service).
- The customer service department needed to be easily contactable.
- Staff should be knowledgeable.
- They should speak clear English.

Do you agree with this wish list? What would be top of your list?

Accurate information

Customers need accurate information. If you are working in customer services, it will not be possible to know everything. Rather than give wrong information to a customer, it is much better to say you don't know but you will find out. It gives customers confidence when staff have good knowledge about a company's products and procedures.

Speed of response

Nobody likes being kept waiting. Excellent customer service means making sure that customers are attended to quickly. Many companies set standards for customer services.

Tesco has a "one-in-front" policy – if there is more than one customer in front of you as you wait to pay, the store opens another checkout. Many companies set response standards for dealing with customer enquiries. These are a typical set of standards:

- answer the phone within seven rings
- return a call within one working day if a message is left
- reply to letters and faxes within 10 working days
- acknowledge emails within 24 hours and respond fully within five working days.

Getting through to the right person

It is the responsibility of the member of staff answering the telephone – often the switchboard operator or the receptionist – to put calls through to the right person. This shows how everyone in a company is involved in customer service to some extent. It is very annoying when customers are put through to several people before they find someone who can help them. In a store, have you ever asked a question to be told: "I don't work on that section." All staff must help customers and, if they cannot, they should quickly find a person who can be of assistance.

Attitude

Customers want service that is pleasant and friendly. If staff seem bored or uninterested, even if they still solve the problem, they will create a bad impression. Customer service will seem poor. Staff must show a positive attitude, and be happy to deal with every customer's enquiry or problem.

The car rental company

Read this account of one person's experience with a car rental company before tackling the activities that follow.

> I was going on a business trip from London to Edinburgh and I decided to hire a car. I booked the car on the Internet with no problem. Then the date of my trip changed and I had to change my booking.
>
> I telephoned the hire car company on the customer services number. I held for 25 minutes before there was an answer. Once I was connected I was put through to sales. I needed customer service to change a booking. I had to ring in again.
>
> This time I only waited 10 minutes and was put through. The agent said I could change my booking but would have to pay £10. I agreed. I was giving my card details to pay when she said: "Oh no. It is not £10, it's £25." I said I would only pay £10 as that was her first quote. She became quite rude and said: "Take it or leave it." I left it!

Working in pairs, identify all the things that went wrong and write them down.

Then role play the scenario as described: one of you acts the part of the customer, the other plays the part of the customer service agent.

Discuss with your partner how to improve this service. Role play the exchange between the customer and the hire company again, but this time the customer service agent should show excellent service.

Just Checking

* What should you do if you don't know the answer to a customer's question?
* What is a one-in-front policy?
* What attitudes would give a poor impression to customers?

Functional Skills: Speaking

In the role play, you will respond appropriately to others and take part in a formal exchange with another person.

Topic 4.6 How is effective customer service provided?

Let's Get Going

Think about a job or work placement you have had. What customer service training did you receive? Hold a discussion with the rest of your group and compare the training you each received. Decide which companies you think gave the best training and why.

In the last section, you looked at some of the features of excellent customer service. So how do companies make sure that they provide good customer service?

Training

If staff are not trained, how will they know how to provide good service? Most companies provide induction training. This training is for staff that have just joined the company. It provides an introduction to the company and its procedures, and usually covers basics on customer service.

Staff may also be offered more specialist training at regular intervals. Some of this training will be on customer service procedures and techniques. Staff will be expected to complete any training course, and are often given a certificate when they have done so. They may even get a formal qualification such as an **NVQ** in Customer Service.

NVQ A National Vocational Qualification.

Incentive A prize or gift to persuade someone to take action.

Monitoring customer service

Companies must constantly monitor and evaluate customer service. This is necessary so that they can make improvements as needed. Table 4.2 sets out some of the ways that this monitoring can be done.

Method	Description
Observation	Managers and supervisors are responsible for checking that staff follow the right procedures. They can watch staff when they are dealing with customers and make sure that they are polite, friendly and give accurate information.
Mystery customers	Staff may behave differently towards customers when they know that they are being watched by managers. To find out the true picture, some companies employ mystery customers (or mystery shoppers). They visit shops or phone up asking for information. They then report on the customer service they receive.
Questionnaires and feedback forms	Many businesses try to get feedback from their customers. Shops may have forms for shoppers to complete. In hotels there is often a questionnaire about service in the room. Sometimes a company offers a prize draw as an **incentive** for customers to fill in questionnaires.
Setting and checking quality standards	Businesses may set standards to keep a high level of service. Examples include setting the maximum waiting time in a queue, answering the phone within a given number of rings, and replying to a letter with a set number of days.

Table 4.2: Methods of monitoring customer service

Staffing levels

Businesses must ensure that there are sufficient staff to deliver effective customer service. If there are too few staff, then it can be really difficult to provide good service. Managers must decide how many staff are needed in **peak periods**, as well as the right staffing levels for slack periods, and plan accordingly.

Peak periods The busiest times for a business.

Merchantable quality Of a quality suitable to be sold.

Confidentiality The act of keeping information private.

Legal obligations

A company must know about and comply with all relevant legislation. There are several Acts of Parliament that protect the customer. The Trades Descriptions Act requires businesses to ensure that products and services are described correctly, and that they are fit for their purpose and of "**merchantable quality**". The Consumer Protection Act makes it illegal to mislead consumers about price. The Data Protection Act requires businesses to hold any information about customers securely and to respect customer **confidentiality**.

Did you know?

It should take a passenger less than 10 minutes to get through a security check at an airport. The queues for security checks are monitored to see exactly how long it takes people to get through at any time.

At your work placement or a company you work with, find out if (and how) the business gets feedback from its customers. Report back to your group. Use visual aids if you can.

Just Checking

* Think of an incentive to encourage someone to come to school or college.
* What does a mystery customer do?

Topic 4.7 The importance of providing effective customer service

So far you have considered what makes good customer service. You have also looked at the steps companies take to achieve effective customer service. But why is this so important? It is said that dissatisfied customers tell seven people on average about their complaint. This negative publicity can discourage other people from doing business with a company. You now need to consider how good customer service benefits a company.

Let's Get Going

Before you start this topic, try to come up with your own ideas in small groups. What are the different benefits that good customer service brings to a business? Share your ideas with the whole class.

Business benefits

All parties should benefit from good customer service – it will mean less complaints and less bad publicity so customers should be satisfied and businesses should prosper. Let's look at the main business benefits.

Building customer loyalty

When customers are happy with the service they get, they are likely to become loyal customers. This means that they may come back to that company again and again. This is known as repeat business.

Attracting new customers

People tell others about their experiences. If you are planning to buy some product or want a service, you may ask friends if they can recommend a good business. Good customer service means positive reports to friends and family. It can lead to recommendations and that can lead to new customers. By building a reputation for excellent service, a company improves its public image and attracts new customers.

Contributing to financial success

So, as has been shown, good customer service contributes to keeping existing customers, attracting new ones and creating a good public image. This has an obvious financial benefit. It allows a business to keep sales and profits at a healthy level, making for a successful organisation.

First Direct

This is an extract from a First Direct leaflet. The leaflet explains how the bank puts customers first.

Putting you first makes all the difference

If you could join a bank that gives customer service absolute priority, who'll treat you with respect, who you'll feel genuinely happy to deal with... and who'll give you £100 just for switching... why wouldn't you do it straightaway? Just open a 1st Account with us before 31 December 2008, conditions apply, and we're certain you'll be better off in every way.

You'll always get through to a real person

Who wants to talk to a machine? When you call 0800 24 24 24 you get to speak to a pleasant, informed human being, in the UK, at any time of the day or night, 365 days a year. In banking terms, this makes us exceptional.

Switching is painless with Easyswitch

Once you've decided to make the move, our Easyswitch team will do all the work for you, liaising with your existing bank to ensure a smooth changeover on an agreed date. It couldn't be simpler.

Activity 4

Choose a company that you know well, perhaps one you have worked with. Produce a leaflet that explains how your chosen company provides customer service. You should use suitable IT to design and make your leaflet.

Functional Skills: ICT

You will be developing, presenting and communicating information when you design your leaflet.

Just Checking

Insert these words into the appropriate spaces in the sentences that follow.

negative   repeat   First Direct   loyal

_________ customers result in _________ business.

When people tell others about a bad experience, a company gets ________ publicity.

The bank ________ believes in putting the customer first.

Topic 4.8 Dealing with customer enquiries

In this section you will find examples of some common routine enquiries that come into businesses. You will practise dealing with these enquiries.

Let's Get Going

Think about the last time you personally made an enquiry or a purchase. Was it face to face, by telephone, mail or email? How was it handled? Did you get good service? Share this experience with your group.

Types of enquiry

Five common types of customer enquiry are considered below. Each type is illustrated by an example.

Activity 5

Asking for information about a product or service

Meena's birthday is coming up. She wants to hire a private room in your pub to hold a party. She wants a disco, a bar and she wants the pub to provide a buffet. The private room is on the first floor, and Meena wants to know if one of her friends who uses a wheelchair will be able to get up to the room.

Your private room is only available from Sunday to Thursday. This is because a jazz band plays on Friday and Saturday nights. Food can be provided by the restaurant next door, but the customer needs to talk to the restaurant directly. A bar can be provided but Meena must pay the barman. There is no charge for the room as long as there are 50 people. A lift is available for the friend to use.

Work in threes. Take it in turns to reply to Meena. This should be through role play. One person plays the role of Meena, one the person who works in the pub. The third person should watch and comment on how the enquiry is dealt with.

Activity 6

Asking the price of a product or service

Miranda is ordering flowers for a wedding. She wants to know the overall price for a bouquet for a bride, three bridesmaids' bouquets, 10 table arrangements and buttonholes for 15 people. The prices of the flowers are:

Bridal bouquet	£55
Bridesmaid bouquet	£35
Single carnation	£4.50
Table centrepiece	£15

Once again working in your groups of three, take it in turns to give Miranda the prices and work out the total price for her.

Activity 7

Asking for directions to the business

A customer calls you and asks for directions to your business. You are going to find the directions on Google Maps and email the link to the customer. Use the address of your centre for this task and email the link to one of your colleagues.

Activity 8

Asking opening, closing or start times

Mrs Marshall rings up and asks what time your store is open on Sundays. The store is open from 10 am, but customers can only browse and not buy for the first hour. Shopping can start at 11 am and the store remains open until 5 pm.

In your groups of three practise replying to this phone call.

Activity 9

Asking to exchange a product

Jonathan bought a gift for his girlfriend. It is a sweater, which turned out to be too small. He has a receipt and wants to change it for another size.

In your groups of three take it in turns to deal with the exchange.

Functional Skills: Speaking and Listening

Activities 5, 6, 8 and 9 will use your speaking and listening skills when taking part in the role plays.

Functional Skills: ICT

You will access, search for, select and use maps and directions on the Internet and evaluate whether they are suitable for your enquirer.

Just Checking

* Make up a customer enquiry of your own and write it on a card. Each learner should produce a card. Everyone should then select a card and practice responding to the enquiry in their groups.
* Explain to a colleague in your group the typical sorts of enquiries an employee might have to deal with.

Topic 4.9 Making a sale

Face-to-face selling is important to a business. This topic looks at the basic steps involved in making a sale. You will get a chance to practise these steps.

Let's Get Going

Julie works in a clothes shop. She likes working in the shop because she gets discount and she is interested in fashion. But things don't always work out well with every customer, as this example shows. Julie is talking to Sahid, her colleague, and doesn't see the customer right away. When she does see her, this exchange follows.

Julie: "Hiya, just browsing are you?"

The customer: "No, I am looking for a present for my niece who is 16."

Julie: "Buy her one of these underwear sets, they are only a tenner."

The customer: "I don't feel comfortable buying her underwear and I was thinking of spending about £20."

What do you think Julie did wrong?

Steps in making a sale

Any sale involves the salesperson taking a number of steps. Figure 4.5 shows the stages of a sale.

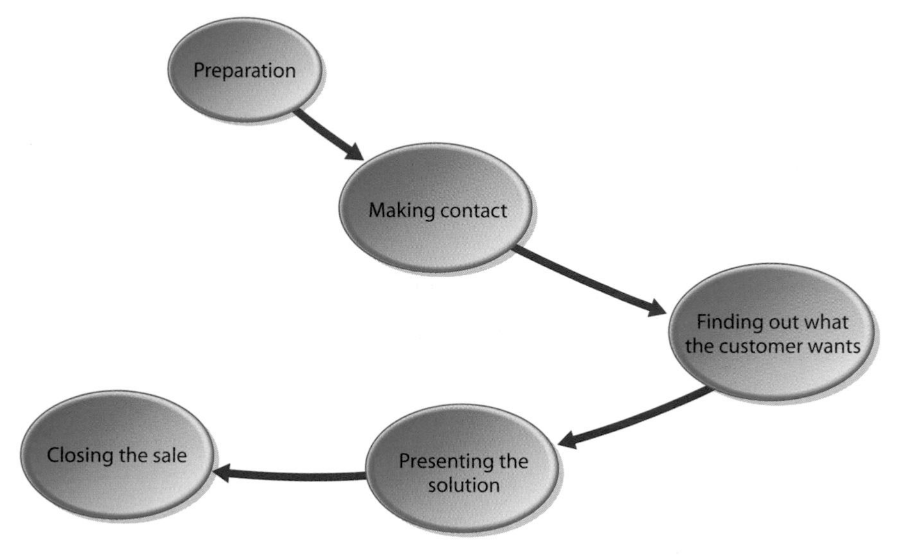

Figure 4.5: The stages of a sale

Preparation

The first thing a salesperson needs to do is good preparation. The importance of product knowledge has been emphasised throughout this unit. If you want to make a sale, you should know all aspects of your products and services. You should know about the product features, about the benefits that products and services offer, and about when they can be delivered. You must know prices. You should learn about any new products and services that your company is introducing. Sales staff prepare by reading information or by taking short training courses on the products.

The physical environment

Wherever you work, you must make sure that areas visited by customers are clean and tidy. If products are on view, they must be clearly displayed. Remember, first impressions count. If you are selling face to face, the customer wants to see a clean and tidy space. If you are in telesales, an organised space or desk helps you stay focused.

Try and find out as much as you can about customers before you meet them. If you work in a shop, you will soon get an idea of your typical customers – whether they are locals or tourists; their age range and income levels.

If you work in telesales, you may have information on your existing customers on file. You can see what they have bought before and how much they paid. Think about how you will approach the customer. How formal will you be? What will you say?

Making initial contact with the customer

You must give a good impression. You should look clean and tidy and approach customers with a smile. As soon as you see customers, greet them in a friendly way. Never ignore a customer while you do something else.

When you are talking to a customer on the phone, sit up straight and smile. Even though the customer can't see you, it still makes a difference. You are trying to **build a rapport** with the customer. This means that they should come to feel comfortable with you and trust you.

Building rapport The process of establishing a positive relationship with someone.

Finding out what the customer wants

This is the hardest part of the sale. Sometimes people are simply not sure what they want! Ask questions to find out the facts. What kind of product do they want? Who is it for?

Ask open questions so that you get more information. **Open questions** begin with words such as "how", "what" and "when". They invite information. **Closed questions** are those which can invite a "yes or no" answer. For example, "is this what you want?" is a closed question. If the customer answers "no", you are not much closer to finding out what they really want.

Open questions
Questions that invite long answers, and typically start with 'how', 'what' and 'when'.

Closed questions
Questions that only invite a limited range of answers, such as yes or no.

It is very important that you listen carefully to answers. You can check you have understood the customer by summarising what they said.

Let's look at an example. Jenny sells flowers over the phone. A customer calls and says he would like to order a bouquet. The following page shows the types of questions Jenny needs to ask to help the customer.

- What occasion are the flowers for?
- How much do you want to spend?
- What particular flowers or colours do you like?

From these questions Jenny will be able to suggest flowers that suit the customer's needs. Then she might ask:

- What message would you like on the bouquet?
- When would you like the flowers delivered?
- How would you like to pay?

Presenting the solution

Now you know what the customer wants, you must show them or tell them about a product or service that meets their needs. You should point out the features and benefits of the product. This is where preparation is really important. If they don't like what you first suggest, find an alternative.

Closing the sale

You have to decide when you think the customer is ready to commit to a purchase. The customer might ask you to confirm the price, ask about delivery times or make a positive remark about the product. Never rush the customer or you might lose the sale. Close by asking how they would like to pay or saying "would you like me to pack this for you?" Sometimes the customer closes for you by saying: "Yes, I'd like that please.'

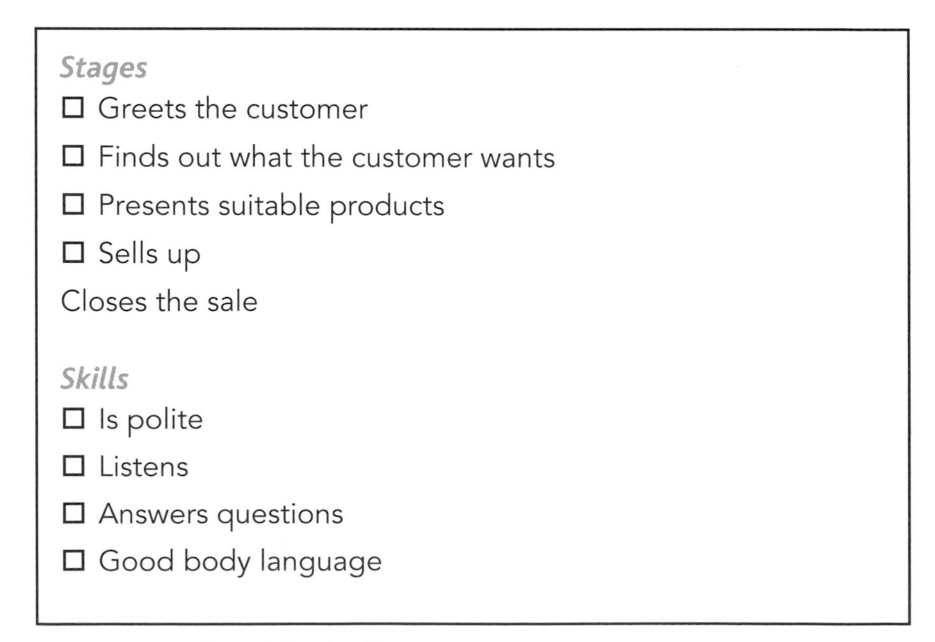

Stages

☐ Greets the customer

☐ Finds out what the customer wants

☐ Presents suitable products

☐ Sells up

Closes the sale

Skills

☐ Is polite

☐ Listens

☐ Answers questions

☐ Good body language

Figure 4.6: Selling skills checklist

Activity 10

This is an activity for your whole group. You are going to set up a mini business and practise your selling skills. It involves a cake sale.

To prepare for the sale, hold a meeting of your group. At this meeting, decide:

- when to hold the cake sale
- where the sale will take place
- what cakes you will have on sale
- what price to charge for each cake
- how to organise any necessary permissions
- how to promote the sale
- who will do what.

Make sure that you provide a wide variety of cakes. You could carry out some initial research to find out what your potential customers would like. You might also find out when is the best time to have a sale. If the cakes are to be sold to students and staff, lunchtime might be best.

Write up your decisions as a plan, listing key times and dates and setting out the resources you will need.

On the day make sure that each person takes a turn in selling. This should be observed by at least one other person so that the seller's skills can be assessed by another person. Assess each other using the checklist in Figure 4.6.

PLTS: Self managers

You will take responsibility for the cake sale and show initiative, commitment and perseverance. You will organise time and resources.

Just Checking

Insert these words into the appropriate spaces in the sentences that follow.

close training rapport leaflets features closed benefits

A sales person can get product information by reading _________ or through _________ .

Building up _________ means establishing a positive relationship.

Pointing out ________ and __________ helps the customer to buy.

The last stage of a sale is the ___________ .

A question that invites the answer yes or no is a ______ question.

Topic 4.10 Skills required when dealing with customers

Many staff can come into contact with customers, not just those in designated sales and customer service jobs. In any customer-facing role there are important skills and qualities that are needed to make it a success.

Let's Get Going

The company that runs Alton Towers invites people to take a quiz on its website to see if they would fit in if they worked at the visitor attraction. Try the quiz by visiting: http://altontowers-jobs.com/would_you_fit_in/

Qualities

In this section you will review the main skills and qualities needed by any staff that deal with customers. Think about whether you have these qualities.

Be positive

Most important is a positive attitude. In sales, this means believing in your organisation's products and services and having the confidence that you can sell them. You must be smartly presented and approachable. Politeness is also important. If you work in customer service and have to deal with enquiries and complaints, you have to be prepared to take responsibility for helping customers.

Using initiative

If you are asked a question or given a problem, then use your **initiative**. This means trying to find out the answer or solve the problem yourself. You do your best to help the customer. However, if you know that the problem or enquiry is too much for you to handle, then find a supervisor or manager that can help the customer.

Communication skills

Good communication skills are key in serving customers. This doesn't only mean giving information but listening too.

Listening

Are you a good listener? How do you know if someone is a good listener? A good listener will:

- keep eye contact
- face the speaker
- make regular responses, such as yes, hum or a nod
- not interrupt unless appropriate.

Activity 11

Practise your listening skills. Work with a partner. Get your partner to speak for a minute about anything that interests them. You should listen using the behaviours described in the bullet points. Try this again, but this time do not listen properly. Yawn, be distracted, look away. Ask the speaker what difference this behaviour makes. Then swap roles, so that you become the speaker and your partner takes the role of the listener.

Ability to give information

You may know all you need to know about the products and services, but you need to be able to communicate this information. You need the ability to pass this knowledge on in the right way to the customer. This may require written (letters and emails) and spoken (face-to-face) communication skills.

Business communications are investigated in Unit 2. Letters are the most formal way of communicating. A business often has standard letters to deal with different enquiries and complaints. Email is less formal but is often used to give information in answer to a customer enquiry.

If you are answering questions or explaining something to a customer, your tone of voice is important. Your tone should show that you are being polite and interested. You should speak clearly and not too quickly. Of course, your style may change a little with different types of customers. For example, if you are speaking to children, you can be less formal but you must still be polite.

Non-verbal communication skills

People don't just communicate through written and spoken language. **Body language** also sends a message to the people we are with. The way that someone stands and behaves tells other people about what they are feeling.

Good body language to adopt when meeting customers includes:

- standing or sitting up straight
- smiling
- making eye contact
- showing that you are listening
- not eating, drinking or chewing gum.

Body language
The way people communicate what they feel through their use of posture, hands and facial expressions.

Initiative The process of trying to find solutions to problems yourself rather than relying on others.

Did you know?

Research (see Figure 4.7) shows that the tone of voice we use and our body language communicates more than the words we use.

Having positive body language helps you build up a rapport with the customer. It makes you look like a professional. You should also learn to notice the body language of customers. You should be able to tell if they are relaxed or tense. Their tone of voice will tell you if they are angry or upset. This will help you deal with them in the right way.

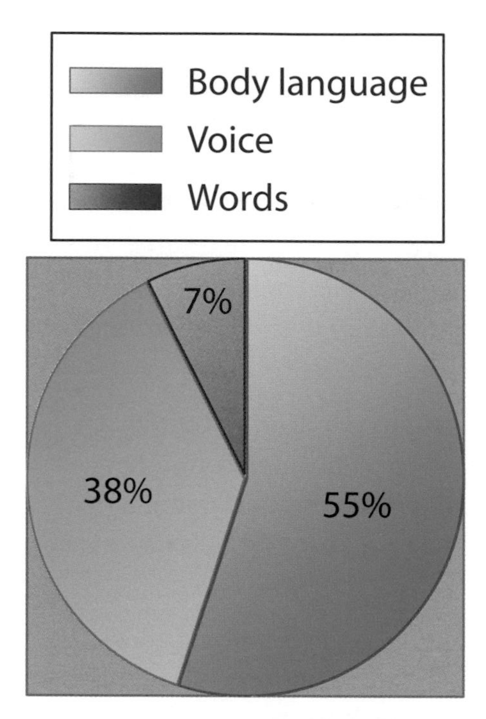

Figure 4.7: How we communicate

PLTS: Reflective learners

You will be assessing yourself and other learners in Activity 12.

Activity 12

Carry out a self-assessment. Score yourself 1–5 on the skills and qualities listed in the first column of the table: 1 is poor and 5 is very good. Discuss your scores in a small group. Do your colleagues agree with your assessment?

Skill	Rating				
	1	2	3	4	5
Listening					
Giving information clearly					
Writing letters					
Writing emails					
Telephone skills					
Positive body language					
Building rapport					

Receptionist

Cavendish House Dental Practice

Permanent

22 hours per week

£11,577 – £12,678

We have a vacancy for a member of staff to join our team in the dental practice. You will be providing a quality receptionist service, welcoming patients, arranging appointments, taking payments and selling dental sundries.

You will need to show excellent customer service skills, and have good communication and interpersonal skills as you will be dealing with a variety of customers face to face and by telephone who have differing needs.

You must be well organised and be enthusiastic about providing a high standard of customer care. Although training will be offered, it is essential that you can use IT applications.

Figure 4.8: A job advertisement

Activity 13

Read the advertisement shown in Figure 4.8. Write a letter to Cavendish House Dental Practice applying for the job. Make sure you say what skills you have that are suitable for the job. Give examples of where you demonstrate these skills. Make sure the letter is in the correct format.

Just Checking

* What three signs show that someone is listening?
* How do you show positive body language?
* Whish is more formal: email or letter?
* When should you find a manager or supervisor to help you?

Thorntons

This is an extract from a report issued by Thorntons, the chocolate manufacturer and retailer.

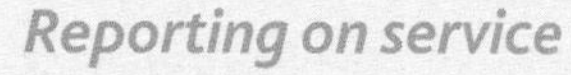

Over the last year we have tried to get a better understanding of our customers.

We have tried to meet our customer needs by improving the products we offer and giving a better customer experience in the shops or online.

Sales over the year have increased due to investment in the improvement of stores, new and exciting product development and imaginative marketing activities.

Financial summary	2007	2006
Revenue	£186.0m	£176.6m
Profit before tax	£7.1m	£5.2m

Thorntons Direct, our online business, grew by 22.9% to £6.8 million. The website has an online servery which allows customers to choose their favourite chocolates in a box design and size to suit their own tastes.

Product development

During the year we successfully introduced new products, Organic truffles and Single Origin Chocolates. It is clear from customer feedback that there is still a healthy demand for old favourites that have been withdrawn from sale. This autumn we will be reintroducing these chocolates and increasing the choice in our larger boxes of Continental from 27 to 53 different chocolates. We are also bringing back a Belgian collection which will be boxed in new and exciting packaging.

We have improved our children's range with new models including princesses for the girls and cars and tractors for the boys, all presented in pink or blue packaging. Parents should know that our high quality products have no artificial colours or added preservatives.

Own store developments

We have made excellent progress with our store refurbishment programme, and 227 stores and cafés have been upgraded. There are new window displays which showcase individual chocolates. In store chocolate fountains are an attraction.

Adapted from Thorntons plc Annual Report 2007.

Tasks

1 Read the case study and use it to answer these questions:
- Where can Thorntons' customers buy the chocolate?
- What special service is offered to online customers?
- How do Thorntons find out what customers want?
- How do models of tractors appeal to boys and parents?
- Find three things mentioned in the case study that might attract new customers.
- Find an example of promoting customer loyalty.

2 What product knowledge and information do you think Thorntons sales staff need? Work in pairs and write down all your ideas. Take it in turns to be the salesperson and the customer, and practise asking each other questions and selling chocolate.

3 Look at the financial figures given for revenue and tax. Work out the percentage change between 2006 and 2007.

4 Imagine you wanted to work at Thorntons. What jobs do you think are available in a store or to run the website? In your pair make a list of the possible jobs. Compare the list with everyone in your group.

5 Now choose one of the jobs you listed in task 4 and think about what skills and qualities that job would need. Write these down. With the help of your partner, assess yourself against these skills and qualities. Set goals for achieving these skills and qualities where you think yours need improving.

PLTS:
Reflective learner

You will assess yourself and your partner in terms of the skills and qualities you have that are suitable for a job. You will set goals for achieving skills and you will invite feedback from a colleague.

Functional Skills:
Mathematics

You will use percentages in an organised way to calculate increases in revenue and profit.

I want to be ...

... a salesperson

Name: Elizabeth Dale

Age: 26

Job: I sell holiday homes on the campsite near where I live in Fréjus in the south of France.

✱ How did you get into sales?

I spent several summers working as a lifeguard on campsites in France. I met people who were selling holiday homes and thought it was an interesting job. About two years ago I asked if I could try it.

✱ Did they give you a job straight away?

No. I had to apply and have an interview. It was hard as I had to speak some French. Then I was given a job just for the summer on trial.

✱ How did you get a permanent job?

That summer I did really well and made some sales so I was offered a permanent job.

✱ What do you like best about your job?

I work outside and get to talk to people all day. And I live on the Côte d'Azur.

✱ What about the money?

I have a set wage and I get commission on sales. The more I sell the more I earn.

✱ What skills and qualities are needed for your job?

To be able to get on with anyone and have good communication skills. My French is good now too. It has improved since I started.

✱ What is the hardest thing about your job?

I have to work all through summer when other people take holidays and the hours are very long. I do get a long holiday in the winter though. The other hard thing is not selling every time.

✱ Would you recommend selling as a job?

Yes, it can be good. It is not office based and you always meet different people. However, you have targets to meet and that can be stressful.

This unit is assessed by an assignment, which is marked by your teacher or tutor.

In order to pass the assignment you must find out about an organisation that sells products and/or services. It will be useful if this is an organisation that you know well and are able to visit. You should be able to outline the sales and customer service functions at this organisation. It will help you if you are able to perform sales and customer service functions yourself in the organisation. The greater the range of functions you are able to discuss, the more marks you will get.

You will identify the customers of the organisation. Try to describe the characteristics of the organisation's main customer groups as clearly as possible, in terms of age, gender, education and income. Say what individual needs different types of customers have.

You must identify the ways in which the organisation provides effective service and describe any areas in which customer service is less satisfactory. Make sure you give specific examples. Link the examples to particular types of customers where you can. The clearer and more specific your examples, the more marks you will get.

You must also explain why effective customer service is important. You can do this by explaining the different benefits of providing effective customer service. If you give very clear reasons and examples you will get more marks.

You will also be assessed on your practical skills in dealing with customers and making sales. You have to be able to deal with routine customer enquiries. You will get more marks if your attitude is positive and enthusiastic and if you are able to answer the enquiries successfully.

When you are making a sale you must show that you have prepared for the sale, with a clean and tidy sales environment and good presentation, and that you have accurate knowledge about products and prices. You should show that you are positive and enthusiastic, with good oral and non-verbal communication. You will get more marks if it is evident that you have detailed knowledge about products and are able to communicate this knowledge to customers.

What you have learned in this unit...

Learning outcome	You should be able to	Summary
LO.1 Know the role of sales and customer services in a business	• outline the functions of sales in a business • outline the functions of customer services in a business	✔In this unit you have learnt about different roles performed by the sales function and the different sales methods that can be used in business. You have learnt about the role of customer services and common customer service procedures.
LO.2 Know how organisations provide effective service to customers	• identify customer characteristics • identify the features of effective customer service	✔You have learnt how customers have individual characteristics and special needs. You have learnt about the factors that differentiate between poor, adequate and excellent customer service. You have found out what organisations do to make sure that they provide effective customer service.
LO.3Understand the importance for organisations of providing good service to customers	• explain the importance to a business of providing effective service to its customers	✔You have learnt why it is important to provide good service to customers.
LO.4 Be able to interact with customers	• prepare for the sales process • communicate with customers in a sales situation • use selling skills to influence others • answer routine customer enquiries	✔You have learnt about the basic steps in making a sale, and the skills and qualities required when making a sale or dealing with customer enquiries. You have practised dealing with routine enquiries from customers.

Careers and Employment in Business

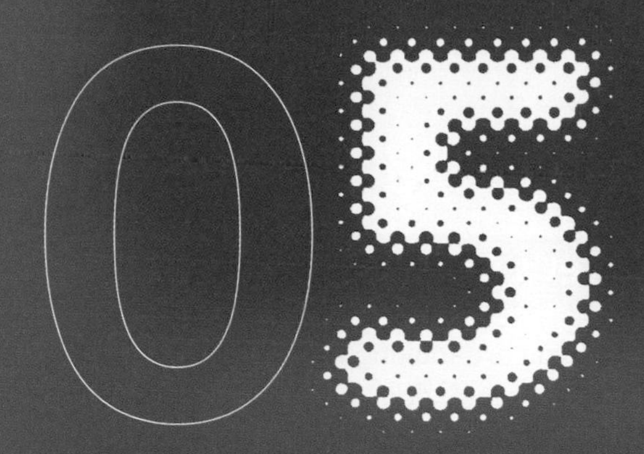

In this unit you will find out about how to use sources of careers information to find a suitable job. You will learn how to make a good impression in written job applications, through the application form, your curriculum vitae (CV) and a covering letter. You will also develop interview skills and learn how to make a good impression at a job interview. The unit will also help you get the most from your work placement. It will help you prepare for the placement and show you how to set yourself achievable goals linked to your placement activities.

What you will learn in this unit

LO.1 Be able to use sources of job information

5.1 Finding out information on jobs

5.2 Researching job opportunities

5.3 Selecting appropriate jobs

LO.2 Know the skills and attributes required in the workplace

5.4 Skills and attributes that will help you succeed at work

LO.3 Be able to prepare for and participate as an interviewee in a job interview

5.5 Completing job application documentation

5.6 Preparing for a job interview

5.7 Taking part in a job interview

LO.4 Know how to set goals for work experience

5.8 Identifying relevant job skills and attributes

5.9 Assessing your strengths and weaknesses

5.10 Setting realistic goals

LO.5 Be able to record and review experiences in the workplace

5.11 Keeping a record of your work experience

5.12 Reviewing your work experience

Assessment

This unit will be assessed by a series of assignments and practical tasks that will be marked by your teacher or tutor. You will need to produce a portfolio of evidence, which will include observation statements and witness statements.

Topic 5.1 Finding out information on jobs

How do you find out about jobs that might be right for you? How do you get to know about job vacancies? In this section you will learn about the most appropriate information sources to use to find a job that is suitable for you.

You can get information about job vacancies from several places. There are many general sources of information about job vacancies including:

- local and national newspapers
- careers advisers
- the Internet
- Jobcentre Plus offices.

If you are looking for a job in a particular field of work you could also try:

- job agencies
- specialist magazines and newspapers.

For example, if you wanted an office job you could contact Pertemps. This is one of several job agencies that specialises in filling part-time and temporary vacancies for office staff. For teaching positions, it would make sense to consult the *Times Educational Supplement*. This is a specialist weekly newspaper for the teaching profession and it has many adverts with job vacancies for teachers. Although it is good to know about these types of specialist sources, when you are starting out, the general sources are more likely to be more useful for you.

Let's Get Going

If you are looking for a job, you need to know where there are vacancies. Sometimes you will see a job vacancy placed in a shop window or a restaurant when a business needs to recruit staff quickly. Can you think of any reasons why this isn't always the best way to find a job?

Job agencies Private companies that help employers fill job vacancies. You apply through the job agency if you are interested in any of the vacancies on its books.

Specialist magazines Publications that focus on particular industries or occupations, such as architecture, education, marketing and human resources. These magazines usually have many advertisements with details of job vacancies.

Figure 5.1: Job centres advertise available jobs for all

Case Study

Richard

Richard gives advice to employers on the best ways to recruit staff. Several employers regularly contact him about where they should advertise their current job vacancies. Suppose you are in Richard's position: where do you think would be the most appropriate place to advertise these vacancies?

Job vacancy	Additional information
Retail assistant	Local supermarket
Marketing manager	Based in London
Bricklayer	Must be willing to travel
Secretary	Temporary position to cover maternity leave
Warehouse assistant	Local branch of national DIY chain

Activity 1

Research the resources available to you in your area by working through this activity.

- **Jobcentre Plus** - Find the address and telephone number of your nearest Jobcentre Plus.
- **Careers advisers** - Research careers advisers in your area. Is there an adviser at your school or college?
- **Local and national newspapers** - Find out the days on which your local and national newspapers publish different job vacancies. Research whether there is any information on jobs and/or vacancies on each newspaper's website.
- **Specialist magazines** - List the best place to find a range of specialist magazines that you could look through for job vacancies. Can these be found in the same place as the newspapers?
- **Job agencies** - List any job agencies that are located locally.
- **Websites** - Research and list any useful websites with information on job vacancies. Visit some company websites and see if there is information on jobs and careers.

Use your research to compile a list of information sources for careers advice and job vacancies. Keep the completed list for reference.

Figure 5.2: A Jobcentre Plus office sign

Just Checking

* Have you made a list of job information sources for reference?
* Have you stored it safely where you can find it easily?

Did you know?

The Connexions service offers advice to young people aged 13–19 about health, relationships, housing, money, work and learning. There are discounts and prizes available for people who sign up for a Connexions Card. You can find out more about Connexions by visiting its website at www.connexions.gov.uk.

Topic 5.2 Researching job opportunities

Let's Get Going

Think about which types of jobs would be suitable for you. For example, if you like working with people, a job in customer service might be more suitable than a job in a factory. Your school or college will have career-guidance software such as Kudos. Use this software package to find out what sort of jobs you are most suited to. Ask for help if you don't know how to use the software.

Now that you know where to look for job opportunities, you can start conducting research into the jobs that are available in your area. It is important that you are realistic about the type of job for which you will be suitable and the pay that you will receive.

Now start researching job vacancies in the types of work that you think will suit you. It would be good practice to use all the six main sources of job information when you conduct this research:

- local and national newspapers
- careers advisers
- the Internet
- Jobcentre Plus offices
- job agencies
- specialist magazines and newspapers.

You will find that getting information on available jobs from a newspaper is a very different experience from walking into a job centre where you may have to ask for help in finding the relevant information. Finding information on jobs from the Internet can be time consuming. You will only know how to get the best out of these sources if you use them.

Figure 5.3: Specialist software like Kudos can help you focus on career choices

John

John is 16 years old and is just about to take his GCSEs. He is unsure about what he wants to do when he leaves school. His teacher suggests that he should have a session on Kudos, the school's career guidance software. She helps John work his way through the questions. The results show that John is suited to a job working with people. This pleases John as he had thought that he might like to work in leisure and tourism. The teacher suggests that John should spend some time researching leisure and tourism jobs and asks him to find two jobs that really appeal to him.

She suggests John gathers as much information as possible on both jobs. They devise a simple grid to record this information.

	Job1	Job 2
Job source		
Company name		
Location		
Job title		
Pay		
Hours		

Table 5.1: A grid to record information on jobs

- Do you think that John's grid is a clear way of recording his findings?
- Use the grid to record your own findings if you think it will present the information you collect on jobs in a clear way.
- Design your own grid if you think that there is a clearer way to present your findings.

Activity 2

Think about the six main sources of information about jobs – newspapers, careers advisers, the Internet, Jobcentre Plus, specialist magazines and job agencies. Which do you think that people regard as being the most useful in helping them find a job? Ask members of your family and close friends which source they think would be the one they would use first if they were looking for a job.

Just Checking

* Have you used all six sources of information for your research?
* Have you been realistic about the types of job opportunities you have been looking for within the case study?

Functional Skills: Using ICT

Using the Internet to find an appropriate job will contribute to your ICT skills. ICT will also be used in Activity 2 to find and select information.

Topic 5.3 Selecting appropriate jobs

Let's Get Going

With your classmates, discuss the types of jobs that you would like to do. How many different jobs has the class thought of?

Hopefully during your research into job vacancies, you found some jobs that might be suitable for you. We suggested that you obtained some basic information about jobs that interest you, such as where the job is located, how much you would earn and how many hours you would have to work. But how should you decide between the jobs on offer?

Activity 3

A careers adviser asks two young people about which jobs they would be applying for when they finished their course.

One says that she would be applying for a supervisor's job in the supermarket where she works on a Saturday morning. The supermarket is a well known national chain which employs over 150 staff at its local store. Supervisors at the store each manage approximately 20 members of staff.

The other says that he would be applying for a full-time job as a firefighter. He had watched a television series about the fire service and thinks that it is an exciting job. He doesn't have any other reason for wanting to join the fire service.

Suppose these two people are the same age as you, and they have similar qualifications and experience to you. Do you think that these are appropriate jobs for these people to be applying for?

List 3 reasons for each person why the jobs are, or are not, appropriate.

There are many reasons why people decide to apply for particular jobs. Some people choose a job because the pay is good. Other people would be prepared to receive less pay if the job was near to their home, or if the job offers prospects to work and build a career in an industry that interests them.

Mothers with small children often choose jobs that fit around school hours. There are people who don't want to work the normal 9–5 working day. They would prefer jobs that offered the opportunity of working **flexitime** or on different **shifts**. Some people prefer to work from home and others want jobs that involve travelling. People who work in retail often say that they like the contact that they have with the public. They would not be happy in a job where they were isolated and had to work alone.

However, some people like to work in isolation and an extreme example would be a lighthouse keeper. This job often involves staying on a lighthouse alone for a number of weeks. As you can imagine, this type of job would not suit everybody. So, there are many reasons why people choose one job rather than another.

Flexitime An arrangement that requires employees to work a given number of hours each week but allows employees some flexibility in choosing the times that they work.

Shifts A system of organising the workforce into different groups so that a business can remain open or operate for longer periods. For example, a company may work a two-shift pattern, say from 6 am to 2 pm, and then from 2 pm to 10 pm. Often, employees work alternate shifts. Half the workforce may work the early shift for a month and then switch to the late shift the following month.

Case Study

Mary

Mary is 60 and she is looking for a part-time job. She has two grandchildren whom she looks after in the school holidays. She has been offered two jobs. The first is in a large supermarket, which is two miles away from her home, the hours are 5 pm to 8 pm Monday to Friday and it pays £6 an hour. She may also have to work Saturdays on occasion. The second job is in a newsagent's at the end of her street. The hours are 10 am to 1 pm Monday to Friday and it pays £7.50 an hour.

- Which job should Mary take?
- Why should she choose this job?

Activity 4

How much do you think you will be earning when you find a job? Let's find out if your expectations are realistic. Get a copy of the local newspaper from the school or college library. Have a look at the job vacancies. Make a list of all the vacancies and record how much pay is being offered for each job.

Just Checking

* Remember that when you are selecting jobs to apply for, they must be appropriate to your age, qualifications and experience.

Functional Skills: Using English

Use your reading skills to compare information on jobs and select the opportunities that are the most appropriate for you.

Topic 5.4 Skills and attributes that will help you succeed at work

Let's Get Going

Who is your favourite teacher or tutor? What is it that makes that teacher stand out from the crowd? Can you identify some of the special skills and attributes that this teacher may have. Here are a couple of examples to get you thinking:

- **skills**
  - always makes the lesson interesting
  - gives me clear feedback on my work
- **attributes**
  - has a good sense of humour
  - is always kind and considerate

Did you know?

Employers place a high value on communication and numeracy skills. They also expect employees to have the ability to work in a team.

Businesses expect their employees to have specific skills and attributes. Some of these will be the same for every job and some will differ and depend on the type of job you are doing. So, what do we mean by skills and attributes? A skill is best described as something that you can do. For example, you might have IT skills or be good at dealing with people (people skills). Attributes are best described as being related to your personality and how you interact with other people. For example, being polite and pleasant to work with is a positive attribute to have in any job situation. Think about these definitions of skills and attributes and the examples we have referred to as you work through this section.

Employers know the specific set of skills and attributes that they expect from employees. Some are job specific: for example, a salesperson who travels to meet different business customers may be expected to be able to drive. However, some skills and attributes are required in every job. They are expected of any good employee. Here is a list of some of these important skills and attributes (and you may be able to think of others):

- good timekeeping
- good presentation and appearance (appropriate to the job)
- a positive attitude to work
- the ability to work in a team
- good communication skills
- information technology skills
- the ability to work with numbers.

Activity 5

Imagine you are working in a newsagent's shop. You have been left on your own in the shop. A customer comes into the shop to complain. She is very annoyed that her newspapers have not been delivered twice this week. The customer is very angry and she is threatening to take her business elsewhere. Make a list of the skills and attributes that would help you handle this situation.

Job skills

A big supermarket chain is opening a huge new superstore in your area. The store will open from 8 am to 10 pm Monday to Saturday and from 10 am to 4 pm on Sundays. Staff would be expected to work different shifts.

A company representative has given a presentation on the jobs that will be available at the store. Two types of job have been identified as particularly suitable for school leavers:

- counter assistants in the store restaurant
- counter assistants in the delicatessen section

The company representative has stressed what the supermarket expects from employees in these two roles. Here is a copy of the PowerPoint slide that was used in the presentation.

Our expectations of you

- Be punctual for work
- Be well dressed and presented
- Able to work well with people
- Display a positive attitude to work
- Able to speak clearly and confidently
- Listens to instructions
- Able to work under pressure

See if you can match your skills and attributes to the expectations of the supermarket. Write a short note stating whether you meet these expectations. Keep your note simple: answer each point with a "yes" or "no", and if you answer "yes" give an example of a situation in which you have shown or used the skill in question. For example, are you punctual? Perhaps you have demonstrated your punctuality at school or college? Do you always arrive on time?

Just Checking

* Have you matched your skills against each of the expectations listed in the case study?
* Have you given an example of a situation in which you have demonstrated each skill?

Functional Skills: Using ICT

Demonstrate your ICT skills by word-processing your answers to the case study and spell checking your results.

Topic 5.5 Completing job application documentation

You need to make a good impression when you are applying for a job and when you get invited for a job interview. This section provides some advice on how to produce a well-presented job application. In the next section, you will consider how to prepare for a job interview.

When you apply for a job it is likely that you will be asked to fill in an **application** form and to include a **curriculum vitae** (CV) with a covering letter. When composing any of the documents to apply for a job you should use the job description or advert. The **job description** will be supplied by the company and will set out the main task and responsibilities of the position. You should try to mention as many of these tasks and responsibilities as possible in your application to prove that you are the best person for the job, and make sure that you provide the potential employer with at least two **references**. All documents in your application will be used by the employer to decide which applicants to invite for an interview. If you are invited for an interview, it means that you have passed the first hurdle.

Let's Get Going

Ask your friends or family members if they have a CV that you can have a look at.

Functional Skills: Using ICT

Your CV will look really professional if you use your ICT skills to produce it on the computer.

Activity 6

Select a part-time job that you would like to apply for. Contact the company advertising the job and ask to be sent further details about the job and an application form. When you receive this, complete the application form. Remember to first check the instructions for filling in the application form and answer all the questions.

Then prepare a CV that you could send with this application form, using a template from your teacher/tutor or the Internet. Finally, write a covering letter to go with the application form and CV.

Functional Skills: Using English

Use your writing skills for the purpose of completing your application form and rewriting Sam's letter.

Activity 7

Figure 5.4 shows a covering letter sent by Sam Smith with a job application. Rewrite the letter to improve its presentation, taking care with the layout, content and spelling.

You need to correct Sam's spelling and his use of full stops. You also need to think about the content. Is "thank you" the correct way to end the letter? Finally check the layout. Are Sam's address and the company's details in the right place?

Hotlink

You can get lots of useful tips about CVs from this website: www.alec.co.uk.

Mr Knight
Wesmans Ltd
100 Broad Street
Newtown
BY10 7PX

Dear Mr Knight

Re-job reference H345

I saw your advert in the paper for an adminstrative asistant. I am 16 and I want to work in an office. I did my work experience at Maxwell's and I liked the work very much I live near your building and I could walk to work I can come for an interview at any time. I like working with people I know how to use a computer. I could start next week.

Thank you,

Sam Smith
26, Milford Rd
Newtown

Figure 5.4: A draft covering letter to go with a job application

Just Checking

* Have you filled the application form in neatly?
* Did you use a template to complete your CV?
* Make sure that your covering letter has no mistakes.

Job application form Many businesses send people a form to complete when they apply for a job.

Curriculum vitae A record of a person's qualifications and experience. Usually shortened to CV.

References People who are prepared to back up someone's job application with a short statement about the applicant's skills and abilities. People usually ask previous employers or teachers/tutors if they will supply references on their behalf.

Job description A short statement about a job, setting out the main tasks and responsibilities of the position.

Topic 5.6 Preparing for a job interview

Let's Get Going

Think about what you should wear for a job interview. Remember that you never get a second chance to make a good first impression. Make a list of "what to wear" and "what not to wear". Include, if appropriate to you, accessories and jewellery as well as clothes.

If you get invited to a job interview, it will mean that you have passed the first hurdle in the recruitment process. Your application will have made a good impression. This is your reward for spending time preparing the documentation for your application. The next step is to prepare for your interview. Companies will normally invite a number of candidates along for an interview when they have a vacancy, so you are likely to be competing with other candidates for the job that you have applied for. It is reasonable to assume that all the other candidates will have done their preparation for the interview. If you prepare thoroughly it will increase your chances of being successful and getting the job. Preparing for an interview does take time but it is time well spent and it may give you that extra selling point that impresses the employer. This topic will help you learn how to prepare effectively for an interview.

Figure 5.5: Dress to impress, first impressions are important

There are several steps you should take to prepare for an interview. Don't leave preparation to the last minutes; these steps are all best undertaken before the day of the interview as last minute preparation is rarely very effective.

- Find out some information about the employer. For example, what does the business make or sell? Who are its main customers? How many people does the business employ? You may get the opportunity to use this information in the interview. The interviewer will be impressed that you have done research on the company.
- Make sure that you know how to get to the company's premises. Plan your journey and allow yourself plenty of time. Arriving late and flustered will not create a good impression.
- Plan what you will wear at the interview. You should aim for a neat, clean and tidy appearance in order to make a good impression.
- Prepare questions that you want to ask about the job. Questions relating to pay, hours and working conditions are good examples of questions you can ask.
- Prepare answers to possible questions that you may be asked at the interview. For example, the following are very typical job interview questions:

Why do you want to work for this company?

Tell me what you learned from your work experience placement.

What are your interests and hobbies?

Why are you leaving your current job – what do you like/dislike about it?

Activity 8

Work with a classmate and identify a company that you would both like to work for. Individually conduct some research to find out five pieces of information about the company. Compare your lists and discuss how you could use your information at the interview to impress the interviewer.

Functional Skills: Using English

Practise the questions you want to ask at the job interview with a friend. In doing so, you will be practising your spoken English skills.

Case Study

Amy

Amy is 16 and she has just left college having successfully completed the Edexcel Business, Administration and Finance Diploma at Level 1. She wants to work in a bank and has found three jobs that appeal. She has submitted application forms for each job. In the post this morning she gets a letter inviting her for an interview for one of the jobs. It is with a large bank that has a branch on the high street of Amy's home town. The job is for a service and sales assistant. The hours are 9 am to 5 pm. It is 37 hours per week and it involves work on Saturday morning. Work in small groups and help Amy prepare for the interview.

- Make a list of questions that Amy could ask about the job.
- Make a list of the possible questions that Amy might be asked at the interview.
- Prepare some model answers to the questions that you think she might be asked at the interview.
- Share your answers with the rest of your class.

Just Checking

Remember the importance of the 2 Ps at interviews.

* Prepare your questions.
* Prepare your answers.

PLTS: Independent enquirer

When you are identifying questions that you may be asked, you will be demonstrating the skills of an independent enquirer.

Topic 5.7 Taking part in a job interview

Let's Get Going

Remember that first impressions are important. Can you think of three things that will help you to make a good first impression at your interview? Compare your ideas with a classmate.

You've impressed an employer enough with your application to have convinced the business that you're worth meeting in person and they have invited you along for a job interview. Now it's a matter of making the best impression in a face-to-face situation. Some people are naturally very good in job interview. They are usually relaxed and confident and they come over well. Other people are not so comfortable in interview situations and they have to work hard to create a good impression. However, everybody can learn, practice and develop the skills that will help them to feel comfortable and confident at job interviews. If you can develop good interview skills your chances of landing a job will be much improved.

On the day of the interview you should be well prepared. Don't worry too much if you feel al little nervous as this is quite common. When you are being interviewed it is important that you give out the right signals. Reflect on how you look and how you sound to the interviewer.

How you sound

The style, **tone** and delivery of your voice are important at an interview. Try not to talk too fast or too quietly. This can be difficult when you are nervous and it sometimes helps to take a deep breath before you start to answer a question. Rehearse your answers beforehand and get a friend or family member to check your speed and tone. Don't use slang and watch out for too many "ers" and "ums". Never cover your mouth when you are speaking. Practising beforehand, especially in front of someone else, can help you identify any bad habits.

How you look

You also need to consider your **non-verbal communication** – the signals that you are giving through your **body language**. For example, how you walk, sit and act is all part of the impression you create.

- Sit reasonably upright; don't slouch in your chair.
- Don't flap your hands. Rest your hands on the table or on your lap.
- Make good eye contact with the interviewer but don't stare.

Figure 5.6: Remember the importance of good body language

- Try to relax, smile and appear confident.
- Don't fidget. Avoid playing with you hair, scratching your nose and shuffling your feet.

Activity 9

Work with a small group of classmates. Each member of the group should take a turn at giving a short presentation. When it is your turn, give a short talk (about two minutes) on a topic of your choice to the group. Ask the group to give you feedback, especially on your speed and tone of delivery.

Functional Skills: Using ICT

By preparing an e-mail you will be demonstrating your ability to communicate electronically.

Case Study

Ahmed

Ahmed is a friend of yours who recently moved to another part of the country. He is 16 and he has just left school. He did his work experience in the office of a timber importing company. He did photocopying and filing, he answered the phone and was shown how the company's online ordering system works. Ahmed enjoyed his work experience and decided that he would like to work in an office.

You received an e-mail from Ahmed today. He told you that he has had three interviews for junior office positions but had not been successful. He thinks that his written applications are good but his interview skills let him down.

Give Ahmed some help. Prepare an e-mail to send to John giving him some tips on how to be successful at an interview. Keep it simple and straightforward. Use headings, such as "What to do" and "What not to do".

Non-verbal communication Communication without the use of (spoken or written) words.

Body language The way people communicate what they feel through their posture, hands and facial expressions.

Voice tone The sound and expression used when speaking. For example, someone might have a soft voice, a stronger loud voice or an angry tone.

Just Checking

* Remember the importance of body language.
* Don't forget to speak clearly in a job interview.
* Remember that you are trying to make a good impression.

Topic 5.8 Identifying relevant job skills and attributes

Your work placement will provide an opportunity to work with new people, learn about different jobs and develop your skills. Good preparation is key to getting the most from your placement.

Your work placement may be your first experience in the world of work. Even if you already have a part time job the experience of being in a placement will be very different for you. You will be working a full day for every day of your placement, probably Monday to Friday on a 9 to 5 basis. You will be working in a different environment with new people and are likely to be given jobs that you have not tackled before. For example, if you are working in an office you could be asked to operate expensive machinery such as photocopiers or you could be asked to do manual or computerised filing work. You may have to deal with situations that you have not experienced previously. For example, if you are working in a retail outlet you may have to deal with an awkward or angry customer for the first time. It is never possible to predict every task that you could be asked to do on a placement nor every type of situation that you are likely to experience. However, you should be as well prepared as possible. Good preparation will help to make the placement an enjoyable and successful experience. If you are well prepared you are much more likely to make that all-important good impression.

Your work placement is designed to give you the opportunity to learn from your experience in the workplace. There are many benefits to be gained from a successful work placement.

- A successful work placement will boost your confidence.
- If you impress the employer you will get a positive reference that you can use when applying for a permanent job.
- You will have gained practical knowledge of what it's like to be part of the workforce and you will have learned the importance of good timekeeping and attendance.
- You will recognise the importance of teamwork.
- It will help you decide if you are suited to a particular type of work.
- You can pick up new skills.
- You can talk to people who are already doing the job and ask them about their experiences of working in this occupation.

Let's Get Going

Go back to the job skills case study in topic 5.4. Have another look at how you matched against the skills and attributes that the supermarket expected from its counter assistants. Would your answers still be the same?

Figure 5.7: Employers expect you to have a positive attitude to work

- A good report from your placement gives you something positive to talk about at a job interview. This will allow you to sell yourself and impress the interviewer.
- Sometimes employers will offer permanent jobs to people who have impressed on placement.

Activity 10

See if you can fill the gaps with the correct word. They are all important points to remember when on your work placement.

When I am on work placement I must arrive on ______ each morning. It is very important that I ______ appropriate clothes. I know how important it is for me to make a good __________ on my placement. If I don't know what to do I must ____ my supervisor or another employee. When my supervisor is giving me instructions I must ________ carefully and I should always have a _________ attitude to my work even if I am given a job that I don't like doing. I will learn to work as part of a _______ because it is important that I can work with other people.

Case Study

Work placement preparation

You will have made contact with your work placement provider and you will have an idea of what you will be doing during the placement. You may have met your supervisor. You will also have some knowledge about the company. This will help you in deciding what skills and attributes are going to be important for you on this placement.

- Make a list of the things that will make you a good employee in your work experience placement. Try labelling them with a S for a skill and an A for an attribute.
- Give an example of why each skill and attribute will be important on your placement. Write a little note on why you think they are important or how you will use them.
- When you have finished, compare your findings with a classmate.

Just Checking

- Remember the importance of making a good impression on your placement.
- Have you included all the skills and attributes that will be appropriate to the placement?

Topic 5.9 Assessing your strengths and weaknesses

Let's Get Going

Think about a relative in your family, such as an aunt, uncle or cousin. What do you really like about this relative? Is there anything that you don't really like? See if you can turn these "likes" and "dislikes" into strengths and weaknesses. For example, if your aunt always brings you presents, you could see her generosity as a strength. If she expects you do the things that she asks immediately, you could see her impatience as a weakness.

One way that you can prepare well for your work placement is to assess your current skills and attributes. Which skills you are satisfied with and which ones need to be improved? This requires that you take an honest look at yourself. This isn't always an easy thing to do.

Before you set goals for your work placement you need to identify your strengths and weaknesses. Table 5.2 has some examples to get you thinking. You will see that many things can either be strengths or weaknesses.

Strengths	Weaknesses
Always arrives on time	Often turns up late
Always listens to instructions	Sometimes gets muddled with instructions
Good telephone manner	Lacks confidence on the phone
Always works hard	Often wastes time
Works well in a team	Doesn't like working with others
Asks questions when confused	Doesn't ask questions when confused
Looks smart	Looks scruffy
Communicates well with anyone	Struggles to communicate
Has a positive attitude	Can be negative

Table 5.2: Some work-related strengths and weaknesses

Did you know?

Being able to identify your own weaknesses is actually a strength.

Activity 11

Your work placement will be an important experience. You will want to make a good impression.

- Identify the strengths that will help you have a successful work placement.
- Identify the areas that you know you will need to improve for your work placement.

Check these out with your teacher or tutor. Does your teacher or tutor agree with your choices?

Imran

Here are some extracts from Imran's work placement diary. His placement was at a supermarket.

Monday

Arrived ten minutes late.

I didn't know how to stack the sliced bread on the shelves so I asked my supervisor. She watched me put the bread on the shelves and she said that it was perfect. Wow.

Tuesday

I had to work with Danny today. He always winds me up but I ignored him.

Wednesday

My supervisor asked me to rearrange the iced buns and the custard slices in "sell by" date order but I thought she said the currant buns and the egg custards. She wasn't happy with me. I was on my own in the bakery and the bakery manager phoned. He wanted to know if the flour had arrived and I was able to tell him. He said that I had been very clear and very helpful.

Thursday

I overslept again this morning. I didn't have time to find a clean shirt, have a wash or comb my hair.

Friday

I forgot to tell them I was going to be late today as I had to go to the dentist. I helped a customer find the bread rolls. She said that I was a polite and well-spoken young man.

These are the strengths and weaknesses that Imran identified before going on work placement.

My strengths:
- I am a good timekeeper
- I am a good listener
- I am always well dressed

My weaknesses:
- I am not confident talking to people
- I don't always listen to what people are saying
- I argue with people that I don't like

Was Imran's self-assessment accurate? Give an example from the case study to show where he was accurate. Give an example form the case study to show where he wasn't accurate.

Just Checking

- ✱ Remember that we all have areas for improvement.
- ✱ Have you included all your strengths?
- ✱ Identifying a weakness is the first step to improvement.

Topic 5.10 Setting realistic goals

You will want to gain some positive experiences from your work placement and develop some of your skills. Setting yourself realistic **goals** is the last piece of the jigsaw in preparation for your work experience. In this topic you will learn the importance of setting yourself goals that are realistic and achievable on your work placement. If you set yourself goals that are unachievable or are unrealistic, you are only likely to get disheartened. So, if you want to make a success of your placement you will need to be realistic in the goals that you set yourself.

What goals do you want to achieve from your work placement? The goals you set could be very simple and straightforward. You may wish to link them to areas you feel you might be able to improve. For example, if you do not have a good record with your timekeeping in school or college then you might want to make "arrive at my placement on time every day" one of your goals. Another way of looking at your goals is to think about what you are good at. You could use the work placement to provide you with proof of this strength. For example, you might say that although timekeeping at school or college was poor, you always arrive on time for your part time job. Your goal could still be "arrive at my placement on time every day". Try to come up with a realistic set of goals for your placement.

Let's Get Going

When he was a small boy, Richard Branson was asked what he wanted to be. He said that he wanted to be a successful businessman. This was probably a realistic goal because he was very focused and he was prepared to work hard to achieve his goal. However, if Richard Branson had said that he wanted to be the owner of a large company like Virgin by the time he was 14 years old, would this have been a realistic goal?

Did you know?

Although David Beckham now seems very confident, he was actually quite shy when he first went to Manchester United. After he got married he became famous not just as a footballer but also as a celebrity. He wasn't used to so much media attention and had to set himself realistic goals on how to handle interviews and how to be photographed. It seems that he has achieved his goals.

Figure 5.8: David Beckham's goal when he was a boy was to play for Manchester United

Activity 12

Have a look at Table 5.3. These set out the goals of four 16 year-olds. Do you think each goal is realistic and achievable? Give your reasons.

Current circumstances	Goal
Working in a supermarket	To be a supermarket manager when I am 30
Working in a hotel	To work hard and get promotion
School leaver with 2 GCSEs	To be a brain surgeon
School leaver with 4 GCSEs	To get a job as a junior office clerk

Table 5.3: The work goals of four young people

PLTS: Reflective learner

When you are thinking about the areas that you need to improve in order to set your work placement goals, you will be practising the skills of a reflective learner.

Functional Skills: Using English

Use your speaking and listening skills to explain how you have chosen your goals with your teacher or tutor and respond constructively to any suggestions.

Emily

Emily is going to work in a hotel on her placement. When she has more experience she wants to be a hotel manager. The hotel has offered her a placement in which she will work with its receptionist for two weeks.

Emily has visited the hotel prior to the placement and has discussed her placement with the receptionist. They have agreed on the things that Emily will be doing. Emily has compiled a list of her strengths and the areas where she thinks she needs to improve.

Emily's strengths:

- I learn quickly.
- I get on well with people I don't know.
- I dress well and I think that personal hygiene is very important.

Emily's weaknesses:

- I sometimes fool around and don't behave sensibly.
- I am not confident in unfamiliar situations.
- I can waste time and be easily distracted.

Can you suggest some realistic and achievable goals for Emily for her work placement?

Just Checking

* Are your goals realistic?
* Have you talked them through with anybody?

Goal Targets that you want to achieve over time or during a particular activity.

Topic 5.11 Keeping a record of your work experience

You should have put in a lot of time in planning and preparing for your work placement. It is likely to be the first time that you have worked as a full-time employee. To help you learn from this experience, it is important to keep an accurate written record of your work placement.

Keeping a work placement diary is the best way to record your work experience. It helps you to keep track of the valuable experiences that you will have on your work placement and the skills you might gain. You should use your diary to record:

- the name of your placement employer
- details of your supervisor
- your work placement dates
- details about the jobs that you are given and how well you coped
- the skills that you practised, such as telephone skills
- things that you learned
- what you enjoyed the most, and why
- what you enjoyed the least, and why
- any feedback you receive from colleagues, other staff and customers.

Let's Get Going

Think about what you did yesterday. Make a list of the main things you did. Take it out again later. Can you add anything you had forgotten about when you made the list. Can you think of any reasons why it is important for you to keep a written record?

Functional Skills: Using English

Record your experiences every day in your diary in a clear and detailed manner. This will allow you to demonstrate your writing skills and will help you to practise dealing with questions that require long answers.

Did you know?

Work experience placements have been the starting point for many successful businessmen and businesswomen.

Activity 13

Make a diary entry for your day at school or college today. Here are some questions you might consider.

- What have I done today?
- What have I learned?
- What have I liked and why?
- What have I disliked and why?
- Who have I met and talked to?
- What did we talk about?

Compare your diary entry with a classmate.

Monique

Monique has just completed the first day of her work placement. She is working in a pet shop. She jotted down some rough notes to write up her diary at home that evening.

I arrived on time and met my supervisor. I met the four shop workers. I liked Helen, she was friendly. Cleaned out the rabbit hutches, smelly, didn't like it. Helen showed me how to stack wild bird food on the shelves. Helen went home before lunch with toothache. Jane came to look after me. We tidied up the storeroom.

After lunch I watched Sarah serving in the shop. She let me serve a customer. I liked doing this, but I got a bit muddled with the customer's change. I asked Sarah for help and she was nice. I helped Beryl with the Christmas window display. She said that I had been a great help. I had to answer the phone because everyone else was serving customers. I forgot to take the caller's name.

- Did Monique learn any new skills today?
- What should she record in her diary for today?

Figure 5.9: You will meet many different people and have new experiences to record in your work placement diary

Just Checking

Remember, entries in your diary will be easier if you:

* do the work you have been given
* observe what goes on
* talk to other employees.

Topic 5.12 Reviewing your work experience

Let's Get Going

Think about an example where you were given some feedback. How did you respond?

Feedback
Information given to a person about their performance, usually by a supervisor or manager.

Did you know?

Body language can be a way of giving informal feedback to friends or to colleagues at work. For example, a frown would be negative feedback but a smile would be a positive response.

Functional Skills: Using English

When you swap diaries about your work experience with a classmate you are practising your reading skills.

It is very important that you learn from your experiences in life. For example, if someone takes a driving test and fails on their reversing skills, they should have learned that they need more practice at reversing the car before they retake the test. They will need to listen to the **feedback** that they receive from their driving instructor and try to respond by improving their reversing skills. In much the same way, you need to review and learn from your experiences on work placement and then respond positively to all feedback.

You will learn a lot from your experiences of working in a different environment. So, you will need to think about what you have gained from the placement experience. Once your placement is over, take a look back at your work placement diary. Think about how well you have done and identify the things that didn't go so well. For example, did anyone praise you for something that you did? Did you learn any new skills? Did you do something that you thought went really well? It is also important that you are honest with yourself when you are thinking about the things that didn't go so well and to think about what you might need to do to improve your performance. Your placement employer should also give you feedback and this may be verbal while you are on placement and written in the form of a placement report back to your teacher/tutor. This employer feedback will be a very useful source of information which you should consider carefully. It is important that you are able to learn from the feedback that you receive about your performance. It is a big confidence boost when you get positive feedback but you also need to reflect on any negative feedback and learn where you need to improve.

Activity 14

Pair up with a classmate and swap work experience diaries. Can you identify the things that went well and the things that could have gone better for each other? This will show you both how accurate you have been in recording your experiences.

Harry's work placement

Harry had a one-week placement in the office of the local council. This is the written feedback he has received from his supervisor.

> **Supervisor feedback: Harry**
>
> Harry is a very pleasant young man. He works well with everybody. He is punctual and always looked very smart. Harry completed all the tasks we asked him to do accurately. He always asked for advice and guidance. He has a very pleasant manner when dealing with members of the public. However, he can be easily distracted from what he is doing and sometimes it took him a long time to complete basic tasks. For example, he was sent on an errand to our other office. It was over an hour before he returned as he had met some friends. He wrote telephone messages down very clearly and carefully. He is very attentive and listens carefully to everything that he is asked to do. He sometimes likes to play around and tell jokes and isn't always aware that this isn't always appropriate in an office environment. Harry helped me to input some data on the computer and he clearly has good IT skills.
>
> We wish Harry well and hope that he is able to find a suitable job when he finishes his course and that he has a very successful career.

- What do you think of Harry's feedback?
- Can you identify the positive points that the supervisor is making about Harry's performance?
- Does the supervisor highlight any areas that Harry should give some thought to and try to improve?

Just Checking

* Have you reviewed your diary records?
* Have you added the details of your work placement to your CV?
* Have you had any feedback from your work placement supervisor?

PLTS: Reflective learner

If you give some careful thought to your work placement feedback, and learn from constructive criticism, you will be demonstrating the skills of a reflective learner.

Paul is a great football fan and he supports his local club who play in the Premiership. He asked his tutor, Mr Taylor, if he could have his work placement at the club. Mr Taylor made several phone calls and followed this up with a letter to the club requesting a work placement. This was followed up with a meeting between Mr Taylor and Mr Evans, the administration manager at the football club. They spent two hours discussing and agreeing Paul's work placement programme. Mr Evans then sent a letter to Mr Taylor confirming the details of the work placement programme.

When Paul arrived at the club for his placement he was met by Mr Evans who showed him around the ground. Paul was very excited as he had never been behind the scenes at a football club before. He was very impressed with the facilities, especially the executive boxes, the fitness suite and the players' dressing rooms. Mr Evans also showed Paul the trophy cabinets. He let Paul hold the FA Cup, which the club had won the previous season.

Mr Evans then took Paul to the club office where he was introduced to Jane who was to be his supervisor for the week. Jane had a copy of the Paul's work placement programme and had been busy arranging tasks for him to complete during the week. They confirmed that one of Paul's goals was to practice his good communications skills.

The club was playing a UEFA Cup game on the Wednesday evening and demand for tickets was high. Paul spent Monday and Tuesday working in the ticket sales office. He answered the phone and helped with enquiries from fans who wanted tickets for the match. Fans also travelled to the ground to buy tickets and Paul was asked to talk to them when they arrived and to direct them to the ticket office. He was really proud to be acting as an ambassador for the club.

On Wednesday, the match programmes arrived from the printers. Paul's job was to sort them out into bundles of 1,000 for the programme sellers. Jane explained that the programmes cost £2 each and they would expect each seller to collect £2,000

Figure 5.10: The football stadium where Paul did his work experience

Functional Skills: Reading

In this case study you will read, understand and extract information to answer the questions.

from programme sales. So it was important that the number of programmes in each bundle was correct. On the night of the match, Paul was part of the team who welcomed people and showed them to their executive boxes. He also helped to check the money from the match programme sales and add up the value of any unsold programmes. A big bonus for Paul was that he was able to watch the match.

Paul spent the next two days in the office. He was asked to input some data into a spreadsheet on the match receipts from Wednesday's game. Jane took him with her to a marketing meeting with the club's sponsors. She asked him to practise taking some notes on what was discussed and they compared their notes afterwards. On Friday, Jane carried out a risk assessment of the football stadium. This involved completing over 100 forms and it took all day. Jane carried out the risk assessment and filled in the forms. Paul was asked to keep all the forms in order so that they could be filed correctly. Paul really enjoyed his placement.

Tasks

1. How many people were involved in arranging Paul's placement?
2. How much time do you think they all spent in making his placement a success?
3. What skills did Paul practise or learn on his placement?
4. Did he achieve his goal?

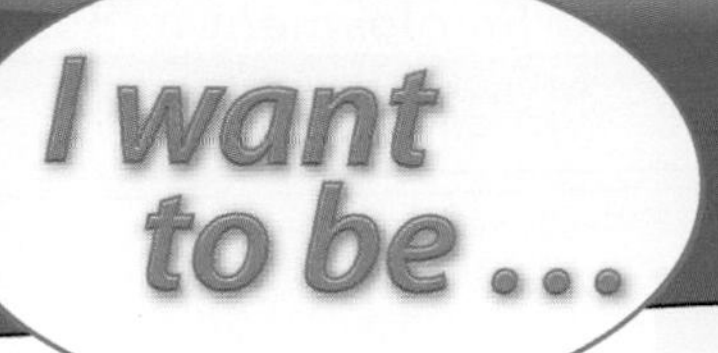

... a human resources officer

Name: Ian Sullivan

Age: 22

* **What do you do in human resources?**

We deal with a whole range of issues relating to staff at the company. For example, we are responsible for advertising vacancies, recruitment and selection, and staff training.

* **What is it like working in an office?**

I love it. There are six of us in our office, three men and three women and we all get on really well. We work very closely together as a team and we always help each other out. Teamwork is important in an office especially if you are working to deadlines.

* **When did you become interested in working in human resources?**

I was really lucky. When I was at college, I did a work placement in the human resources office at the local council. I really enjoyed it and this inspired me to work hard at college so that I could gain my qualifications.

* **What is the best part of your job?**

That's a difficult question. The job is quite varied and I get to do a lot of different things. At the moment I am involved in helping to organise some computer training for our office staff. We have to contact training providers and decide who we will hire to do the training. I really enjoy contacting people and discussing our requirements with them.

* **What is the hardest part of your job?**

Probably the fact that we have to meet deadlines all the time. However, this keeps us on our toes and helps to make the job interesting.

* **What qualifications do you need?**

It depends at which level you come in. I started as an office junior to get some experience. I then applied for an administrative post in a human resources department and I was able to get some "on-the-job" training, which enabled me to build on my qualifications.

* **What skills do you need?**

You need to have good IT skills as we spend a lot of time on the computer. You also need to be able to work well with other people. You have to be reliable and you need to be positive and enthusiastic about your work.

This unit is assessed by an assignment, which is marked by your teacher or tutor. This section will give you some ideas and guidance on the sort of things that will help you pass this unit.

Your work experience is a very important part of this unit. You should choose two jobs that are related to your career plans. For example, if you want to work in retail, try to find two jobs in different areas of retail such as a clothes shop and a supermarket. This will give you more scope for ideas when you are comparing the two job opportunities. When comparing jobs, the obvious things to look at are wages, hours and holidays. However, to make a really impressive comparison you should also take account of working conditions and career opportunities.

To cover learning outcome 2 you will need to identify skills and attributes required in the workplace. One of the ways to do this is to talk to people in work. If you have a part time job, talk to your supervisor and ask them what skills they expect their employees to have. If you have a speaker from business coming in to talk to your class, ask them the same question.

When learning about application documents and interviews, treat it as if you are applying for a real job and it will improve your performance. Make sure that the format of your letter is correct and watch your spelling and grammar. Get someone to check your documents before you hand them in. Try to relax at the interview as this will increase your confidence. Get someone to help you practise your interview questions before the interview.

The key thing with setting goals for your work experience is that they need to be realistic and achievable. They don't have to be big goals. In fact, it is often much better if they are simple and straightforward. The important thing is that they relate directly to your needs on your work experience.

When you are completing your work placement diary make sure that it has enough detail to allow you to make an assessment of your experience. You need to be honest in your assessment of your work experience as your placement provider will also be providing feedback on your performance. When you are responding to the feedback from your work experience supervisor, think about the comments before you respond. Your answer will be much more balanced if you do this, especially if some of the feedback is not positive.

What you have learned in this unit...

Learning outcome	You should be able to	Summary
LO.1 Be able to use sources of job information	• find out job information • compare job opportunities	✔In this unit you have explored the different sources of information about jobs and careers: ✔careers advisers ✔company websites ✔job agencies ✔Jobcentre Plus ✔newspaper and magazines ✔careers guidance software.
LO.2 Know the skills and attributes required in the workplace	• identify skills and attributes required at work	✔You have learned about skills and attributes that will help you succeed at work, such as: ✔good timekeeping ✔appropriate presentation ✔the ability to work in a team ✔good communication skills ✔information technology skills ✔the ability to work with numbers.
LO.3 Be able to prepare for and participate as an interviewee in a job interview	• communicate information in job application documents • identify questions to answer in preparation for the interview • communicate as an interviewee	✔You have learned about the preparation and process involved in a job interview: ✔CV preparation ✔interview protocols ✔preparing questions ✔communication skills ✔non-verbal communication skills.
LO.4 Know how to set goals for work experience	• set goals for work experience	✔You should have identified skills and attributes that are relevant for your placement, and which of these you feel you need to concentrate on most.
LO.5 Be able to record and review experiences in the workplace	• assess how successful work experience has been • interpret feedback received during work experience	✔You have learned how to use a work experience diary and how to reflect on your experiences on completion of your placement.

Useful websites

www.adviceguide.org.uk
Citizens Advice Bureau provides information and advice on money and debt.

www.bankofengland.co.uk
Has information on bank notes, including features to counteract fraud.

www.businessballs.com
Team building activities.

www.dwp.gov.uk
Department for Work and Pensions gives guidance on benefits and entitlements.

www.hse.gov.uk
The Health and Safety Executive website has information on various issues of health and safety in the workplace.

www.jobcentreplus.gov.uk
The government website dedicated to jobs.

www.moneyfacts.co.uk
Looks at the best ways to save and invest.

www.moneymatterstome.co.uk/interactive-Tools
Allows you to calculate interest on savings and loans.

www.nationaldebtline.co.uk
Provides free and confidential advice about dealing with debt problems.

www.royalmint.co.uk
Shows UK coins and notes produced, including special editions.

www.winspiration.co.uk/positive.htm
Includes a section on positive words that could be used in presentations.

Glossary

agenda a list of the topics to be discussed at a meeting, setting out the order in which they will be covered.

body language the way people communicate what they feel through their use of posture, hands and expression.

break even in sales, if you receive enough money to cover your costs this is when you break even.

budget shortfall when you have spent more money than planned so don't have any left.

budget surplus you have more money than anticipated because your expenses are lower than planned.

building rapport establishing a positive relationship with someone.

channel the means by which a product or service reaches (or is sold to) the customer.

close bringing the customer to a buying decision.

closed questions only invite a limited range of answers, such as yes and no.

cold calling making sales call (or visits) at random to people who have not previously expressed interest in your product.

concessions price discounts offered to particular groups, such as the elderly, the unemployed or students.

confidentiality the act of keeping information private.

curriculum vitae a record of a person's qualifications, experience and skills. Usually shortened to CV.

entrepreneur someone who is able to recognise opportunities for new products, services and processes or ways to make improvements to existing products, services and processes. Entrepreneurs need to be creative, brave and prepared to work hard.

feedback information given to a person about their performance, usually by a supervisor or manager.

flexitime an arrangement that requires employees to work a given number of hours but allows employees some flexibility in choosing the times that they work.

formal communication based on an organisation's needs and business requirements. Formal communication channels are normally regulated and/or planned by the organisation. An example is confirming a customer order by letter.

functional area a specific business function, such as customer service, human resources and production. A functional area could be the responsibility of an individual, a section or a department.

gender grouping people by sex: that is, male and female.

goal targets that you want to achieve over time or during a particular activity.

incentive a prize or gift to persuade someone to take action.

income the money received by a person (or household) from their work, benefits, pensions and other sources.

informal communication communication channels based on the needs of individuals and groups. They can satisfy social needs and usually develop spontaneously. An example is a casual conversation with a colleague.

initiative the process of trying to find solutions to problems ourselves rather than relying on others.

interest free credit a payment plan that allows customers to pay for their goods in regular instalments over a period of time without paying any interest.

interpersonal skills needed to communicate with and relate to other people effectively.

jargon terminology, often buzzwords, relating to specific activities or groups. Jargon can be a barrier to effective communication. It can also be used to show you are a member of a group or to exclude others.

job agencies private companies that help employers fill vacancies.

job application form many business ask applicants to complete a form when applying for jobs.

job description a short statement about the job, setting out main tasks and responsibilities.

house style the rules and standards for the design and writing of documents.

market the target customer group for a product or service. A product might be targeted at children aged 7 to 11, girls aged 14 to 16 or men in their 30s. These are all examples of markets.

memory stick a removable storage device that plugs directly into a computer through a USB port.

merchantable quality of a suitable quality to be sold.

minutes a written record of a meeting. Minutes list the names of people attending, summarise the discussions and any decisions taken and set out anything that need to be done following the meeting.

mobility the ability to get around.

motivation the driving force that makes you act the way you do. The energy you put into an activity is related to what you expect to get out of it.

non-verbal communication communication without the use of the written or spoken word.

NVQ a National Vocational Qualification.

open questions questions that invite long answers, and typically start with how, what and when.

peak periods the busiest times for a business.

potential customer someone who might buy a product or service.

product an item offered for sale.

profit the difference between the money received from sales of products and services and the money spent on running the business.

references people, usually previous employers or teachers, who are prepared to back up someone's job application by providing a short written statement about the person.

response rate the percentage of people receiving a direct mail who reply to it.

revenue the amount of money coming into a company through sales.

service something available for use by a customer.

shifts a system of organising the workforce into different groups so that a business can operate for longer hours or around the clock. Some staff may work early, late or nights shifts, eg. 0600–1400, 1400–2200, 2200–0600.

specialist magazines publications that focus on particular industries or occupations such as architecture, education, marketing and human resources.

stakeholder an individual or group of people who have an interest in a particular business or organisation. A company's stakeholders include its customers, supplier, employees and the local community.

voice speed the rate at which someone speaks – that is, how slowly or quickly.

voice tone the sound and expression used when speaking. For example, a voice may be soft, strong or loud, or have an angry tone.

work placement diary a method of recording your experiences in the workplace.

Index